INSTRUCTOR'S RESOURCE MANUAL

to accompany

Gaetz / Phadke

THE WRITER'S WORLD
SENTENCES AND PARAGRAPHS
THIRD EDITION

Julie Nichols
Northwest Florida State College

Prentice Hall

Upper Saddle River Boston Columbus Indianapolis New York San Francisco
Toronto Amsterdam Cape Town Dubai London Madrid Milan Munich Paris Montreal
Tokyo Delhi Mexico City São Paulo Sydney Hong Kong Seoul Singapore Taipei

Instructor's Resource Manual to accompany Gaetz/Phadke, *The Writer's World: Sentences and Paragraphs, Third Edition*

Copyright © 2011, 2009, 2006, Pearson Education, Inc.

ISBN 10:   0-205-78181-0
ISBN 13: 978-0-205-78181-2

Prentice Hall is an
imprint of

www.pearsonhighered.com

TABLE OF CONTENTS

The Instructor Resource Center has the entire Instructor's Resource Manual available for downloading in addition to the Text Answer Key. Instructions on obtaining these downloadable resources can be found on Page xi.

Developmental Writing Student Supplements

Q: Would your students benefit from additional exercises that offer both practice and application of basic writing skills, with direct links to additional online practice at MyWritingLab.com?
The Pearson Lab Manual for Developing Writers (Sentences 0-205-63409-5/ Paragraphs 0-205-69341-5/
Essays: 0-205-69340-7)
This three-volume workbook is an ideal supplement for any developmental writing sequence. References direct students to Pearson's MyWritingLab, the marketing-leading online practice system, for even more practice.
- **Volume A: Sentences (0-205-63409-5)**
At this level, exercises and applications of grammar, punctuation and mechanics stress rules rather than simply skill and drill. There are many composing exercises that apply sentence skills explained in the students' primary textbook.
- **Volume B: Paragraphs (0-205-69341-5) & Volume C: Essays (0-205-69340-7)**
The exercises encourage students to apply key concepts covered in most writing classes—i.e. topic sentences, thesis statements, coherence, unity, levels of development. *Analysis* exercises give further illustration of concepts explained in class and in the primary textbook; *Building* exercises give students the "raw materials" to develop paragraphs and/or essays along the various modes. Revision prompts encourage students to look at specific key elements of their own writing and assess whether they have met the needs of their reading audience.

Q: Would your students benefit from having real student essays and quality student models?
The Pearson Student Essays Booklet (0-205-60544-3)
This brief booklet of student models includes two essays from each of the nine modes. It also includes an essay that showcases the writing process from beginning to end, crystallizing the importance of revision for all writers.

Q: Are your students visual learners? Would they benefit from exercises and writing prompts surrounding various images from everyday life, art, career, education?
Pearson Visual Writing Guide for Developing Writers by Ileen L. Linden (0-205-61984-3)
The Pearson Visual Writing Guide for Developing Writers is a thematic supplement designed to stimulate reading comprehension through an authentic perspective of visual imagery. Each assignment challenges the learner to think beyond the text to the image, expanding their worldview as they navigate through complex or unfamiliar issues. This approach teaches deconstruction, a problem-based strategy that reveals important social and cultural interrelationships across the curriculum. Instructors will find this a practical guide for assignments directed toward journaling, reflection, argumentative essay writing and more.

Q: Do you require your students to have a portfolio? Would a daily/monthly/yearly planner help them to get organized?
The Pearson Student Planner (0-205-66301-X)
This unique supplement provides students with a space to plan, think about, and present their work. In addition to the yearly planner, this portfolio includes an assessing/organizing area, daily planner for students including daily, weekly, and monthly calendars, and a useful links page.

Q: Do you require your students to keep a writing journal, and would students benefit from prompts and exercises within the journal to help guide their writing? Would a planner included directly in this journal help keep them organized through the semester?
The Pearson Writer's Journal and Student Planner by Mimi Markus (0-205-64665-4)

This supplement gives students a place to explore their own writing in the writer's journal section while also giving them space to stay organized in the student planner section. The journal portion of the supplement guides students' writing through prewriting strategies, suggested themes for their journal writing, and sample student entries. In the planner section, students can use the monthly, weekly, and daily calendars to effectively manage their time and their course assignments.

Q: Would your students benefit from seeing how writing is relevant to a range of careers?
Applying English to Your Career by Deborah Davis (0-131-92115-0)
This supplement includes a brief page of instruction on 25 key writing skills, followed by practice exercises in these skills that focus on seven specific career fields.

Q: Would you like help in providing your students with more grammar and mechanics exercises?
Eighty Practices by Maxine Hairston Emerita (0-673-53422-7)
A collection of ten-item exercises that provide additional practice for specific grammatical usage problems, such as comma splices, capitalization, and pronouns.

The Pearson Grammar Workbook, 2/e by Jeanette Adkins (0-131-94771-0)
This workbook is a comprehensive source of instruction for students who need additional grammar, punctuation, and mechanics assistance. Covering such topics as subject-verb agreement, conjunctions, modifiers, capital letters, and vocabulary, each chapter provides helpful explanations, examples, and exercises.

The Pearson ESL Workbook, 2/e by Susan Miller and Karen Standridge (0-131-94759-1)
This workbook is divided into seven major units, each of which provides thorough explanations and exercises in the most challenging grammar topics for non-native speakers of English. Topics include nouns, articles, verbs, modifiers, pronouns, prepositions, and sentence structure.

Q: Do you have your students evaluate their peers' work? Would you like them to have an evaluation guide to help them review for their work and the work of their classmates?
What Every Student Should Know About Practicing Peer Review (0-321-44848-0)
Michelle Trim

Q: Do you have your students work in groups? Would you like them to have a guide to maximize the group work?
Learning Together: An Introduction to Collaborative Learning by Tori Haring-Smith (0-673-46848-8)
This brief guide to the fundamentals of collaborative learning teaches students how to work effectively in groups.

Q: Would you like help in providing your students with more editing exercises?
- **Print: Pearson Editing Exercises (Student / 0-205-66618-3, Instructor Answer Key / 0-205-66617-5)**
The Editing Exercises booklet contains fifty one-page editing paragraphs that provide students with opportunities to learn how to recognize and correct the most common types of sentence, grammar, and mechanical errors in context. Embedding the errors within the context of informative paragraphs rather than using discrete sentence exercises simulates a more natural writing situation, allowing students to draw upon their intuitive knowledge of structure and syntax, as well as specific information from class instruction. The booklet makes an ideal supplement to any grammar, sentence, or writing text. Various editing topics can be assigned to coordinate with class lessons, or they may be assigned individually based on problems observed in students' writing. Students may also complete selected exercises as an enrichment activity, either on their own or in collaboration with other students. Additionally, the variety of topics in the paragraphs themselves can also be used as springboards for discussion or journaling, or as models for writing assignments if desired.
- **Online: MyWritingLab APPLY exercises**
Get students reviewing and responding to students' paragraphs. Go to www.mywritinglab.com for more information.

Q: Would you like help in providing your students with more writing assignment topics?
100 Things to Write About Ron Koertge (0-673-98239-4)
This brief book contains over 100 individual writing assignments, on a variety of topics and in a wide range of formats, from expressive to analytical writing.

Q: Do you assign a research paper? Would students benefit from brief guides explaining specific aspects of research?
What Every Student Should Know About Researching Online (0-321-44531-7)
David Munger / Shireen Campbell

What Every Student Should Know About Citing Sources with APA Documentation (0-205-49923-6)
Chalon E. Anderson / Amy T. Carrell / Jimmy L. Widdifield, Jr.

What Every Student Should Know About Citing Sources with MLA Documentation (0-321-44737-9)
Michael Greer

What Every Student Should Know About Avoiding Plagiarism (0-321-44689-5)
Linda Stern

Q: Do you require a dictionary or stress the need of owning a dictionary?
The New American Webster Handy College Dictionary, 3/e (0-451-18166-2)
A paperback reference text with more than 100,000 entries.

Q: Do you require and/or suggest a thesaurus?
The Oxford Essential Thesaurus (0-425-16421-7)
From Oxford University Press, renowned for quality educational and reference works, comes this concise, easy-to-use thesaurus - the essential tool for finding just the right word for every occasion. The 528 page book includes 175,000 synonyms in a simple A-to-Z format, more than 10,000 entries, extensive word choices, example sentences and phrases, and guidance on usage, punctuation, and more in exclusive "Writers Toolkit."

Q: Do you require a dictionary and/or thesaurus?
The Oxford American Desk Dictionary and Thesaurus, 2/e (0-425-18068-9)
From the Oxford University Press and Berkley Publishing Group comes this one-of-a-kind reference book that combines both of the essential language tools—dictionary and thesaurus—in a single, integrated A-to-Z volume. The 1,024 page book offers more than 150,000 entries, definitions, and synonyms so you can find the right word every time, as well as appendices of valuable quick-reference information including: signs and symbols, weights and measures, presidents of the U.S., U.S. states and capitals, and more.

Penguin Discount Novel Program

In cooperation with Penguin Putnam, Inc., Pearson is proud to offer a variety of Penguin paperbacks at a significant discount when packaged with any Pearson title. Excellent additions to any English course, Penguin titles give students the opportunity to explore contemporary and classical fiction and drama. The available titles include works by authors as diverse as Toni Morrison, Julia Alvarez, Mary Shelley, and Shakespeare. To review the complete list of titles available, visit the Pearson-Penguin-Putnam website: http://www.pearsonhighered.com/penguin.

What Every Student Should Know About (WESSKA) Series

The **What Every Student Should Know About...** series is a collection of guide books designed to help students with specific topics that are important in a number of different college courses. Instructors can package any one of these booklets with their Pearson textbook for no additional charge, or the booklets can be purchased separately.

What Every Student Should Know About Preparing Effective Oral Presentations **(0-205-50545-7)**
Martin R. Cox

What Every Student Should Know About Researching Online **(0-321-44531-7)**
David Munger / Shireen Campbell

What Every Student Should Know About Citing Sources with APA Documentation **(0-205-49923-6)**
Chalon E. Anderson / Amy T. Carrell / Jimmy L. Widdifield, Jr.

What Every Student Should Know About Citing Sources with MLA Documentation **(0-321-44737-9)**
Michael Greer

What Every Student Should Know About Avoiding Plagiarism **(0-321-44689-5)**
Linda Stern

What Every Student Should Know About Practicing Peer Review **(0-321-44848-0)**
Michelle Trim

Multimedia Offerings

Q: Do your students have trouble transferring skill and drill lessons into their own writing or seeing errors in others' writing? • Would you like constant awareness of your students' progress and work in an easy-to-use tracking system? • Would a mastery results reporter help you to plan your lectures according to your class' weaknesses? • Do you want to save time by having work automatically graded and feedback supplied?
MyWritingLab (www.mywritinglab.com)
MyWritingLab is a complete online learning system with *better* practice exercises to make students better writers. The exercises in MyWritingLab are progressive, which means within each skill module students move from literal comprehension to critical application to demonstrating their skills in their own writing. The 9,000+ exercises in the system do rehearse grammar, but they also extend into the writing process, paragraph development, essay development, and research. A thorough diagnostic test outlines where student have not yet mastered the skill, and an easy-to-use tracking systems enables students and instructors to monitor all work in MyWritingLab.

STATE SPECIFIC SUPPLEMENTS

For Florida Adopters:
Thinking Through the Test: A Study Guide for the Florida College Basic Skills Exit Test, by D.J. Henry and Mimi Markus

FOR FLORIDA ADOPTIONS ONLY. This workbook helps students strengthen their reading skills in preparation for the Florida College Basic Skills Exit Test. It features both diagnostic tests to help assess areas that may need improvement and exit tests to help test skill mastery. Detailed explanatory answers have been provided for almost all of the questions. *Package item only—not available for sale.*

Available Versions:

Available Versions:	
Thinking Through the Test A Study Guide for the Florida College Basic Skills Exit Tests: Reading and Writing, without Answers 3/e	0-321-38740-6
Thinking Through the Test A Study Guide for the Florida College Basic Skills Exit Tests: Reading and Writing, with Answers, 3/e	0-321-38739-2
Thinking Through the Test A Study Guide for the Florida College Basic Skills Exit Tests: Writing, with Answers, 3/e	0-321-38741-4
Thinking Through the Test A Study Guide for the Florida College Basic Skills Exit Tests: Writing, without Answers, 3/e	0-321-38934-4

Preparing for the CLAST, 7/e (Instructor/Print 0-321-01950-4)
These two, 40-item objective tests evaluate students' readiness for the Florida CLAST exams. Strategies for teaching CLAST preparedness are included.

<u>For Texas Adopters</u>
The Pearson THEA Study Guide, by Jeannette Harris (Student/ 0-321-27240-4)
Created specifically for students in Texas, this study guide includes straightforward explanations and numerous practice exercises to help students prepare for the reading and writing sections of THEA Test. *Package item only—not available for sale.*

<u>For New York/CUNY Adopters</u>
Preparing for the CUNY-ACT Reading and Writing Test, edited by Patricia Licklider (Student/ 0-321-19608-2)
This booklet, prepared by reading and writing faculty from across the CUNY system, is designed to help students prepare for the CUNY-ACT exit test. It includes test-taking tips, reading passages, typical exam questions, and sample writing prompts to help students become familiar with each portion of the test.

Developmental Writing Instructor Resources

Pearson is pleased to offer a variety of support materials to help make teaching developmental English easier on teachers and to help students excel in their coursework. Many of our student supplements are available free or at a greatly reduced price when packaged with a Pearson writing textbook. Contact your local Pearson sales representative for more information on pricing and how to create a package.

On the Front Lines by Donna Bontatibus (0-205-81680-0)
On the Front Lines is a practical, streamlined guide designed for the instructors—new, adjunct, temporary, and even seasoned—of developmental writing at the community college. Within eight concise chapters, instructors receive realistic, easy-to-apply advice that centers on the preparation and teaching of developmental writing in a nation with over 1,000 community colleges. Instructors will be walked through the process of preparing a syllabus; structuring the classroom experience; appealing to different learning styles; teaching with technology; constructing and evaluating assignments; and conferencing with students. This accessible guide also encourages instructors to look outside the classroom--
to familiarize themselves with campus resources and policies that support the classroom experience--and

to look ahead for their own professional development opportunities. Given the debates on developmental education and the importance of first-year experience initiatives to assist with student transition and retention, there is a monumental amount of weight placed on the shoulders of instructors of developmental writing. *On the Front Lines* respects the instructor's role in the developmental writing classroom and offers practical, straightforward guidance to see the instructor through the preparation of classes to the submission of final grades.

The Pearson Developmental Writing PowerPoints (0-205-75219-5)
To complement face-to-face and online courses, The Pearson Developmental Writing PowerPoint resource provides overviews on all the elements of writing an effective essay. This pedagogically sound PowerPoint guide will provide instructors and students with informative slides on writing patterns – classification, cause/effect, argument, etc. – and common grammatical errors, with questions and answers included.

The Pearson Test Bank for Developmental Writing (Print Version) by Janice Okoomian with contributions by Mimi Markus—available via the Instructor Resource Center ONLY (0-321-08486-1)
This test bank features more than 5,000 questions in all areas of writing. In addition to extensive grammar practice, the test bank covers paragraphs and essays, including such topics as the writing process and documentation. Instructors simply log on to the Instructor Resource Center (IRC) to download and print the tests of their choice.

MyTest for The Pearson Test Bank for Developmental Writing (online only) (0-205-79834-9)
This test bank features more than 5,000 questions in all areas of writing, from grammar to paragraphing through essay writing, research, and documentation. Through this instructor friendly program instructors are able to edit these questions and tests to suit their classroom needs and are also allowed more flexibility to manage assessments at any time.

Diagnostic and Editing Tests with Exercises, 9/e (0-321-41524-8)
This collection of diagnostic tests helps instructors assess students' competence in standard written English to determine placement or to gauge progress.

The Pearson Guide to Community Service-Learning in the English Classroom and Beyond by Elizabeth Kessler Rodriguez (0-321-12749-8)
Written by Elizabeth Rodriguez Kessler of the University of Houston, this monograph provides a definition and history of service-learning, as well as an overview of how service-learning can be integrated effectively into the college classroom.

Instructor Resource Center

Getting Registered

To register for the Instructor Resource Center, go to www.pearsonhighered.com.

1. Click **"Educators"**; the first picture on the left.
2. Click **"Instructor Resource Center"** on the top navigation.
3. Request access to download digital supplements by clicking the **"Register"** button.

Follow the provided instructions. Once you have been verified as a valid Pearson instructor, an instructor code will be emailed to you. Please use this code to set up your Pearson login name and password. After you have set up your username and password, proceed to the directions below.

Downloading Resources

1. Go to www.pearsonhighered.com and use the "Search Our Catalog" option to find your text. You may search by Author, Title, or ISBN.

2. **Select your text** from the provided results.

----

3. After being directed to the catalog page for your text, click the **Instructor** link located under **Resources**.

Clicking the Instructor link will provide a list of all of the book-specific print and digital resources for your text below the main title. Items available for download will have a 📥 icon.

----

4. **Click the highlighted file name** of the version you want to download.

📥 Instructor's Manual (.2MB | zip file | Type: Manuals/Guides) ❓

You will be prompted to login with an Instructor Resource Center login.

----

5. Enter your login name & password, and click the **"Log In"** button.

----

6. Read the terms and conditions and then click the **"I accept"** button to begin the download process.

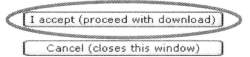

Cancel (closes this window)

----

7. **"Save"** the supplement file to a folder you can easily find again.

The Writer's World: Sentences and Paragraphs, 3rd Edition
Suggested Syllabus: 12 weeks

Week One
Chapter 1: Exploring
Chapter 2: Developing
Chapter 3: Revising and Editing
Chapter 4A: The Illustration Paragraph
Reading 6: "Cultural Minefields," William Ecenbarger
Reading 17: "The Rewards of Dirty Work," Linda L. Lindsey and Stephen Beach
Chapter 6: Nouns, Determiners, and Prepositions

Week Two
Chapter 4B: The Narrative Paragraph
Reading 2: "Birth," Maya Angelou
Reading 10: "The Fire Below," Bill Bryson
Chapter 7: Pronouns
Chapter 8: Subjects and Verbs

Week Three
Chapter 4C: The Descriptive Paragraph
Reading 1: "Fish Cheeks," Amy Tan
Reading 9: "What It Feels Like to Walk on the Moon," Buzz Aldrin
Chapter 9: Present and Past Tenses
Chapter 10: Past Participles

Week Four
Chapter 4D: The Process Paragraph
Reading 14: "How to Handle Conflict," P. Gregory Smith
Reading 15: "How to Remember Names," Roger Seip
Chapter 11: Progressive Tenses
Chapter 12: Other Verb Forms

Week Five
Chapter 4E: The Definition Paragraph
Reading 13: "The Allure of Apple," Juan Rodriguez
Reading 16: "Meet the Zippies," Thomas L. Friedman
Chapter 13: Subject-verb Agreement
Chapter 14: Tense Consistency

Week Six
Midterm Review

Week Seven
        Chapter 4F: The Comparison and Contrast Paragraph
        Reading 3: "The New Addiction," Josh Freed
        Reading 11: "The Zoo Life," Yann Martel
        Chapter 15: Compound Sentences
        Chapter 16: Complex Sentences
        Chapter 17: Sentence Variety

Week Eight
        Chapter 4G: The Cause and Effect Paragraph
        Reading 4: "Fat Chance," Dorothy Nixon
        Reading 12: "Is It Love or a Trick?" Jon Katz
        Chapter 18: Fragments
        Chapter 19: Run-ons

Week Nine
        Chapter 4H: The Classification Paragraph
        Reading 5: "What's Your Humor Style?" Louise Dobson
        Chapter 20: Faulty Parallel Structure
        Chapter 21: Adjectives and Adverbs
        Chapter 22: Mistakes with Modifiers

Week Ten
        Chapter 4I: The Argument Paragraph
        Reading 7: "The Cult of Emaciation," Ben Barry
        Reading 8: "Shopping for Religion," Ellen Goodman
        Chapter 24: Spelling
        Chapter 25: Commonly Confused Words
        Chapter 26: Commas

Week Eleven
        Chapter 5: Writing the Essay
        Chapter 27: The Apostrophe
        Chapter 28: Quotation Marks and Capitalization

Week Twelve
        Chapter 23: Exact Language
        Chapter 29: Editing Practice
        Review and Testing

The Writer's World: Sentences and Paragraphs, 3rd Edition
Suggested Syllabus: 14 weeks

Week One

Chapter 1: Exploring
Chapter 2: Developing
Chapter 3: Revising and Editing
Chapter 4A: The Illustration Paragraph
Reading 6: "Cultural Minefields," William Ecenbarger
Reading 17: "The Rewards of Dirty Work," Linda L. Lindsey and Stephen Beach
Chapter 6: Nouns, Determiners, and Prepositions

Week Two

Chapter 4B: The Narrative Paragraph
Reading 2: "Birth," Maya Angelou
Reading 10: "The Fire Below," Bill Bryson
Chapter 7: Pronouns
Chapter 8: Subjects and Verbs

Week Three

Chapter 4C: The Descriptive Paragraph
Reading 1: "Fish Cheeks," Amy Tan
Reading 9: "What It Feels Like to Walk on the Moon," Buzz Aldrin
Chapter 9: Present and Past Tenses
Chapter 10: Past Participles

Week Four

Chapter 4D: The Process Paragraph
Reading 14: "How to Handle Conflict," P. Gregory Smith
Reading 15: "How to Remember Names," Roger Seip
Chapter 11: Progressive Tenses
Chapter 12: Other Verb Forms

Week Five

Chapter 13: Subject-verb Agreement
Chapter 14: Tense Consistency

Week Six

Midterm Review

Week Seven

Chapter 4E: The Definition Paragraph
Reading 13: "The Allure of Apple," Juan Rodriguez
Reading 16: "Meet the Zippies," Thomas L. Friedman

Chapter 15: Compound Sentences
Chapter 16: Complex Sentences
Chapter 17: Sentence Variety

Week Eight
Chapter 4F: The Comparison and Contrast Paragraph
Reading 3: "The New Addiction," Josh Freed
Reading 11: "The Zoo Life," Yann Martel
Chapter 18: Fragments
Chapter 19: Run-ons

Week Nine
Chapter 4G: The Cause and Effect Paragraph
Reading 4: "Fat Chance," Dorothy Nixon
Reading 12: "Is It Love or a Trick?" Jon Katz
Chapter 20: Faulty Parallel Structure

Week Ten
Chapter 4H: The Classification Paragraph
Reading 5: "What's Your Humor Style?" Louise Dobson
Chapter 21: Adjectives and Adverbs
Chapter 22: Mistakes with Modifiers

Week Eleven
Chapter 4I: The Argument Paragraph
Reading 7: "The Cult of Emaciation," Ben Barry
Reading 8: "Shopping for Religion," Ellen Goodman
Chapter 23: Exact Language
Chapter 24: Spelling
Chapter 25: Commonly Confused Words

Week Twelve
Chapter 5: Writing the Essay
Chapter 26: Commas
Chapter 27: The Apostrophe

Week Thirteen
Chapter 28: Quotation Marks and Capitalization
Chapter 29: Editing Practice

Week Fourteen
Review and Testing

The Writer's World: Sentences and Paragraphs, 3rd Edition
Suggested Syllabus: 16 weeks

Week One

      Chapter 1: Exploring
      Chapter 2: Developing
      Chapter 3: Revising and Editing
      Chapter 4A: The Illustration Paragraph
      Reading 6: "Cultural Minefields," William Ecenbarger
      Reading 17: "The Rewards of Dirty Work," Linda Lindsey and Stephen Beach

Week Two

      Chapter 6: Nouns, Determiners, and Prepositions
      Chapter 7: Pronouns

Week Three

      Chapter 4B: The Narrative Paragraph
      Reading 2: "Birth," Maya Angelou
      Reading 10: "The Fire Below," Bill Bryson
      Chapter 8: Subjects and Verbs
      Chapter 9: Present and Past Tenses

Week Four

      Chapter 10: Past Participles
      Chapter 11: Progressive Tenses
      Chapter 12: Other Verb Forms

Week Five

      Chapter 4C: The Descriptive Paragraph
      Reading 1: "Fish Cheeks," Amy Tan
      Reading 9: "What It Feels Like to Walk on the Moon," Buzz Aldrin

Week Six

      Chapter 13: Subject-verb Agreement
      Chapter 14: Tense Consistency

Week Seven

      Chapter 4D: The Process Paragraph
      Reading 14: "How to Handle Conflict," P. Gregory Smith
      Reading 15: "How to Remember Names," Roger Seip
      Chapter 15: Compound Sentences
      Chapter 16: Complex Sentences

Week Eight

      Midterm Review and Testing

Week Nine
 Chapter 4E: The Definition Paragraph
 Reading 13: "The Allure of Apple," Juan Rodriguez
 Reading 16: "Meet the Zippies," Thomas L. Friedman
 Chapter 17: Sentence Variety

Week Ten
 Chapter 18: Fragments
 Chapter 19: Run-ons
 Chapter 20: Faulty Parallel Structure

Week Eleven
 Chapter 4F: The Comparison and Contrast Paragraph
 Reading 3: "The New Addiction," Josh Freed
 Reading 11: "The Zoo Life," Yann Martel
 Chapter 21: Adjectives and Adverbs
 Chapter 22: Mistakes with Modifiers

Week Twelve
 Chapter 4G: The Cause and Effect Paragraph
 Reading 4: "Fat Chance," Dorothy Nixon
 Reading 7: "The Cult of Emaciation," Ben Barry
 Chapter 23: Exact Language
 Chapter 24: Spelling
 Chapter 25: Commonly Confused Words

Week Thirteen
 Chapter 4H: The Classification Paragraph
 Reading 5: "What's Your Humor Style?" Louise Dobson
 Chapter 26: Commas
 Chapter 27: The Apostrophe

Week Fourteen
 Chapter 4H: The Argument Paragraph
 Reading 7: "The Cult of Emaciation," Ben Barry
 Reading 8: "Shopping for Religion," Ellen Goodman
 Chapter 28: Quotation Marks and Capitalization

Week Fifteen
 Chapter 5: Writing the Essay
 Chapter 29: Editing Practice

Week Sixteen
 Review and Testing

PART II

CHAPTER RESOURCES

The Writer's World: Sentences and Paragraphs, 3rd Edition
CHAPTER 1: EXPLORING
Summary

Chapter 1 begins with a definition of *exploring* and a list of four steps:

- Considering the topic
- Considering the audience
- Considering the purpose
- Exploring strategies

Each of these four steps is explained. Students are first advised to understand the assignment, including length, due date, and special writing qualities. The topic is defined, and special note is made of narrowing the topic and finding an interesting angle. The audience is definedas the intended reader, and students are advised to adapt their language and vocabulary to suit various audiences. A hint box points out that the instructor is the audience for most assignments.

Purpose is explained as the reason for writing: to entertain, to persuade, or to inform. A hint box points out that purposes may overlap.

The majority of Chapter 1 focuses on exploring(prewriting)strategies. A hint box tells when to use exploring strategies: to find a topic, narrow a topic, generate ideas about a topic, or to generate supporting details.

Freewriting is defined as writing nonstop for a limited period of time with no concerns about logical thought, grammar, or spelling. An example of freewriting is presented. In Practice 1 students identify topics from the sample freewriting that have potential for development. The Writer's Desk asks students to choose a topic and freewrite.

Brainstorming is explained as a list of ideas. A student example of brainstorming is presented. Practice 2 asks students to identity ideas from the sample that have potential for development. The Writer's Desk asks students to choose a topic from a list and brainstorm.

Clustering is explained as a word map with lines connecting ideas, and a student example is presented. Practice 3 asks students to choose clusters from the sample that would make a good paragraph. The Writer's Desk asks students to choose a topic from a list and try clustering.

A hint box brings up the questioning method of prewriting: asking *who, what, when, where, why,* and *how* to generate ideas.

There is a short discussion of journal and portfolio writing followed by examples of possible writing topics.

In The Writer's Room, Writing Activity 1 asks students to choose a topic and practice freewriting, brainstorming, and clustering. Writing Activity 2 asks students to view a cartoon and identify the topic, the audience, and the purpose, then brainstorm about possible topics inspired by the cartoon.

Chapter 1 ends with a checklist to remind students of topic, audience, purpose, and exploring strategies.

The Writer's World: Sentences and Paragraphs, 3rd Edition
CHAPTER 1: EXPLORING
Exercises

Set 1: Concepts

1. Which of the following is NOT one of the steps in the writing process?
    a. Think about your purpose.
    b. Proofread and edit your work.
    c. Think about your audience.
    d. Try exploring strategies.

2. When your instructor assigns a topic, you should _____ it to suit your interests.
    a. generalize
    b. exaggerate
    c. narrow
    d. widen

3. When you consider your audience, you consider
    a. who will read your writing.
    b. how much your readers know about your subject matter.
    c. what kind of information your readers will expect.
    d. all of the above

4. When you consider your audience, you also
    a. adapt your tone and vocabulary to suit them.
    b. try to choose very sophisticated words to give your writing more credibility.
    c. attempt to write in a very casual tone.
    d. try to impress the reader by using a thesaurus.

5. In academic writing, your audience is generally
    a. your friends and family.
    b. your co-workers.
    c. the general public.
    d. your instructor.

6. Which of the following is NOT one of the purposes in writing?
    a. entertain
    b. inform
    c. impress
    d. persuade

7. *Exploring strategies* is also known as
  a. research.
  b. paragraph development.
  c. prewriting strategies.
  d. tone.

8. When you freewrite, you
  a. write nonstop for a limited period of time.
  b. make a list of ideas.
  c. draw a word map.
  d. all of the above.

9. When you cluster, you
  a. write nonstop for a limited period of time.
  b. ask *who, what, when, where, why,* and *how.*
  c. make a list of ideas.
  d. draw a word map.

10. When you brainstorm, you
  a. write nonstop for a limited period of time.
  b. make a list of ideas.
  c. draw a word map.
  d. all of the above

11. When you ask yourself *who, what, when, where, why,* and *how* about your topic, you are using which exploring strategy?
  a. freewriting
  b. brainstorming
  c. questioning
  d. clustering

12. When freewriting, if you run out of ideas, you should
  a. stop writing and think for a while.
  b. re-read what you have written and then start again.
  c. take a break and try again later.
  d. repeat a word or phrase or write "I don't know what to say."

13. When you make a list of ideas, you are
  a. freewriting.
  b. clustering.
  c. questioning.
  d. brainstorming.

14. When you use questioning as an exploring strategy, you
    a. ask other people for suggestions for your essay.
    b. look for information on the internet.
    c. ask yourself a series of questions about your topic.
    d. all of the above

15. An effective way to practice writing is to
    a. watch television for ideas.
    b. read comic books.
    c. study the dictionary.
    d. keep a writing journal.

Set 2: Application

1. Virginia's instructor has assigned an essay about athletes. What should Virginia do first?
       a. Begin with an outline.
       b. Ask her friends for ideas.
       c. Understand the length, due date and special writing qualities required.
       d. Begin the first draft as soon as possible.

2. What should Virginia's second step be?
       a. Narrow her topic.
       b. Write an outline.
       c. Write the first draft.
       d. Proofread and edit her freewriting.

3. Juan wants to explain a how computer language works. In his essay for his English instructor, what should he adjust?
       a. the purpose
       b. the length of the essay
       c. the vocabulary
       d. the exploring strategies

4. If Tamika wants to write an email to her supervisor at the bank where she works, which passage represents the most appropriate language vocabulary?
       a. Hey, I need to be off Friday cuz there's this Rob Thomas concert I just gotta see.
       b. Good morning, Mrs. Ferguson. It is my intent to request an 8-hour leave of absence on Friday from my position as teller because of a conflict between my obligation to adhere to personnel attendance requirements and my desire to participate as an audience member during the presentation of a musical performance by singer Rob Thomas.
       c. Hi, mrs. ferguson can i plz have Friday off theres a rob thomas concert that i would like to attend.
       d. Good morning, Mrs. Ferguson. I would like to request a day off this Friday so that I may attend a Rob Thomas concert.

5. Which of the following audiences would require the most formal language and vocabulary?
       a. A letter to a CEO of a major corporation, requesting a position as an intern.
       b. An email to your neighbor asking if she can water your plants while you are out of town.
       c. A note to your sister, asking her to remember to put gas in your car.
       d. An English essay in which you describe your humorous attempt to ride a unicycle.

6. If Ike wants to tell the funny story of his first date, his purpose would likely be to
   a. entertain.
   b. inform.
   c. persuade.
   d. all of the above

7. If Dennis wants to write about how tsunamis form, his purpose would likely be to
   a. entertain.
   b. inform.
   c. persuade.
   d. all of the above

8. If Claire wants to argue that school uniforms should not be forced on students, her purpose would likely be to
   a. entertain.
   b. inform.
   c. persuade.
   d. all of the above

9. Jonah is trying to freewrite, but he keeps getting stuck and can't think of what to write. What should he do?
   a. Repeat the last work or phrase or write "I don't know what to say."
   b. Stop and re-read what he has written.
   c. Take a break and return to his task later.
   d. Review his work and correct the grammar and spelling.

10. Brittany is not having much luck getting ideas while prewriting. She is setting her timer for ten-minute periods and writing whatever comes to her mind. She is being careful to write correctly; she stops and looks up spelling words and checks her punctuation. What is she doing wrong?
   a. She should set her timer for longer periods of time.
   b. She should consider the value of her ideas before writing them down.
   c. She should not stop writing in order to check spelling or punctuation.
   d. all of the above

11. Questioning can be an effective exploring strategy because the questions
   a. help you define and narrow a topic.
   b. provide topic sentences.
   c. are the easiest method of prewriting.
   d. help set the tone and vocabulary.

12. Look at the list of brainstorming items below on food. Which idea is the most narrow, the one that can be the most easily developed within a single paragraph?
   health foods
   fast foods
   vegetables

hidden sugar in fruit juices
meats
desserts
beverages
milk

a. health foods
b. milk
c. fast foods
d. hidden sugar in fruit juices

13. Identify the type of exploring strategy below.
 Who enjoys casinos? Who is opposed to them?
 What are the economical benefits of casinos for our community?
 When would the community see the benefits or the negative impact?
 Where would casinos be located in our community?
 Why would casinos be welcome or unwelcome?
 How can casinos benefit or harm our community?

 a. freewriting
 b. brainstorming
 c. clustering
 d. questioning

14. Identify the type of exploring strategy below.
 casinos—fun gaming
 jobs for locals
 more tourism
 local entertainment
 crime
 gambling addiction
 traffic and parking problems
 seedy reputation for community

  a. freewriting
  b. brainstorming
  c. clustering
  d. questioning

15. Christie is nervous about writing paragraphs for her English class. She has a hard time coming up with ideas, and she wants more practice. What method of writing practice would be the most beneficial to her?
 a. She should sign up for an advanced writing course.
 b. She should write emails to her friends.
 c. She should keep a writing journal.
 d. She should begin writing a novel.

CHAPTER 2: DEVELOPING
Summary

Chapter 2 covers five key steps in the developing stage of writing:

- Narrowing the topic
- Expressing the main idea as a topic sentence
- Developing supporting ideas
- Making a paragraph plan (outline)
- Writing the first draft

Chapter 2 begins with a review of paragraph form and structure, with an illustration of the parts and a sample student paragraph. In Practice 1, students identify the supporting ideas in the student example paragraph. The form of the paragraph, including indentation and margins, is emphasized.

  o In Step 1, narrowing the topic, students are advised to use exploring strategies learned in Chapter 1. An example is provided, and in The Writer's Desk, students practice narrowing five broad topics.

  o In Step 2, the topic sentence is defined as a sentence that expresses the main idea and has several features: it introduces the topic, states the main (or controlling) idea, is the most general sentence, and is supported by other sentences. The controlling idea is explained as the point about the topic and is followed by two examples of topic sentences, the topics and controlling ideas underlined.

In Practice 2, students identify both the topic and the controlling idea in nine sentences. Students are advised to ask themselves four questions to avoid common topic sentence errors:

  o Is my topic sentence a complete sentence?
  o Does my topic sentence have a controlling idea?
  o Does my topic sentence make a valid and supportable point?
  o Can I support my topic sentence is a single paragraph?

In a hint box, students are advised to avoid a topic sentence that expresses an obvious or well-known fact; instead, the topic sentence should be interesting to readers.

In Practice 3, students evaluate and revise six problematic topic sentences. In another hint box, students are advised to place their topic sentence at the beginning of the paragraph. In Practice 4, students choose the best topic sentence for each of three short paragraphs.

In The Writer's Desk, students narrow each of five broad topics, then write a topic sentence that contains a controlling idea.

In Step 3, supporting ideas, three steps in determining a paragraph's supporting details are discussed: generate supporting ideas, choose the best supporting ideas, and organize your ideas. A student example is provided.

Paragraph unity is explained, and students are encouraged to choose ideas that clearly support their topic sentence. A student example of unified points is provided, and a hint box suggests ways to identify the best ideas.

In The Writer's Desk, students choose a topic sentence from their previous Writer's Desk exercise and make a list of supporting ideas.

Three organizational methods for supporting details are discussed: time order, emphatic order, and space order. Time order is identified, and a list of transitional expressions is provided. An example paragraph is provided, and in Practice 5, students use time order to arrange supporting details for two topic sentences. A diagram helps explain emphatic order, and a list of common transitional expressions is provided, followed by an example paragraph. A hint box advises students to use their own values and opinions to determine emphatic order. In Practice 6, students use emphatic order to organize supporting details for two topic sentences. Another diagram is used to illustrate space order. Common transitional expressions are listed, followed by Practice 7, where students read an example paragraph and then answer two special order questions about the paragraph. In Practice 8, students use space order to arrange five details for a topic sentence. In Practice 9, students decide which organizational method best suits each of six topic sentences.

In The Writer's Desk, students review the list of ideas they wrote for a previous Writer's Desk exercise and organize those ideas using time, emphatic, or space order.

Step 4, the paragraph plan, begins with a hint box about adding details that are sufficiently specific. A student example of a paragraph plan is presented. In The Writer's Desk, students review the topic sentence and organized list of supporting ideas created in previous Writer's Desk exercises and complete a paragraph plan.

Step 5, the first draft, begins with a student example that contains some mistakes. In a hint box, suggestions for effective concluding sentences are provided.

In The Writer's Desk, students write the first draft from the paragraph plan they created in a previous Writer's Desk exercise. In The Writer's Room, Activity 1, students select a topic from a list of six and write a paragraph. In Writing Activity 2, students describe their neighborhood.

The developing checklist reminds students to check their work for a topic sentence that introduces the topic and states the controlling idea, to support the topic sentence with facts and examples, to organize the details using time, space, or emphatic order, to ensure that their paragraph plan helps them visualize the main and supporting ideas, and to ensure that their paragraph uses complete sentences.

At the chapter's end, students are directed to the MyWritingLab website for supplemental lectures and additional practice sets.

CHAPTER 2: DEVELOPING
Exercises

Set 1: Testing Concepts

1. Which of the following is NOT one of the steps in the developing stage of writing a paragraph?
    a. narrowing your topic
    b. developing your supporting ideas
    c. making a plan
    d. editing for grammar and punctuation

2. When you narrow your topic, you
    a. look for an aspect of your topic that interests you.
    b. establish your main idea.
    c. write your first draft.
    d. express your main idea.

3. When you organize your main and supporting ideas, you are
    a. narrowing your topic.
    b. developing your main ideas.
    c. expressing your main idea.
    d. making a plan.

4. When you communicate your ideas in a single written piece, you are
    a. finding an aspect of the topic that interests you.
    b. writing your first draft.
    c. organizing your main and supporting ideas.
    d. narrowing your topic.

5. When you write a topic sentence that expresses the main idea of the piece of writing, you are
    a. narrowing your topic.
    b. organizing your main and supporting ideas.
    c. expressing your main idea.
    d. writing your first draft.

6. A group of sentences that focus on one central idea is
    a. a paragraph.
    b. an essay.
    c. a topic sentence.
    d. a report.

7. The first word in a paragraph should be
    a. written in all capital letters.
    b. even with the left margin.
    c. indented ten spaces.
    d. indented five spaces.

8. When you make your topic for a paragraph more specific, you are
    a. developing your ideas.
    b. making a plan.
    c. narrowing your topic.
    d. concluding your paragraph.

9. The topic sentence of a paragraph is one that
    a. expresses the main idea.
    b. provides a transition from one sentence to the next.
    c. provides details that support the main point.
    d. is often placed in the middle of the paragraph.

10. The purpose of body sentences is to
    a. bring the paragraph to a satisfactory close.
    b. provide details that support the main point.
    c. provide a smooth transition from one sentence to the next.
    d. introduce the point of the paragraph.

11. The margins on each side of your paragraph should be
    a. three spaces from the sides of the page.
    b. three inches from the sides of the page.
    c. Half an inch from the sides of the page.
    d. 1 to 1 and one halfinches from the sides of the page.

12. The controlling idea expresses
    a. the general topic.
    b. the most specific topic.
    c. the writer's opinion or attitude about the topic.
    d. the definition of key words in the topic sentence.

13. Which of the following would make an effective topic sentence?
    a. an incomplete sentence
    b. a sentence that has a controlling idea
    c. a sentence that makes an announcement
    d. a sentence that is vague

14. When a paragraph has unity,
   a. all of the sentences are directly related to the topic sentence.
   b. all of the sentences are specific.
   c. the sentences are joined with transitions.
   d. the paragraph is organized.

15. When you use emphatic order to organize the supporting details in your paragraph, you
   a. describe an image in the sequence in which you see it.
   b. arrange the details according to the sequence in which they have occurred.
   c. use exclamation points to emphasize each of your supporting details.
   d. organize your supporting details in a logical sequence.

Set 2: Testing Applications

1. What is the topic sentence in the paragraph below?

Most people think of ski resorts as a winter destination, but they offer many fun activities in the summer as well. When our family stayed in Breckenridge, Colorado, last summer, we took a chair lift to a restaurant at the summit of one of the mountains. We snapped dozens of photographs of the mountain scenery and the bountiful wildflowers on the way up. On the deck of the restaurant, we ate a hearty lunch of delicious hamburgers and homemade French fries. The next day, we rode bicycles along a bike path that wound through beautiful fields and cool forests. The path was fairly flat, so the riding was quite enjoyable. Our best day, however, was the day we went horseback riding through lush green meadows with spectacular mountains in the distance. We all bought cowboy hats and enjoyed a little taste of the Wild West. Next summer, our family plans to travel to another ski resort.

a. Next summer, our family plans to travel to another ski resort.
b. When our family stayed in Breckenridge, Colorado, last summer, we took a chair lift to a restaurant at the summit of one of the mountains.
c. Our best day, however, was the day we went horseback riding through lush green meadows with spectacular mountains in the distance.
d. Most people think of ski resorts as a winter destination, but they offer many fun activities in the summer as well.

2. Which sentence in the paragraph below is NOT a supporting sentence?

Most people think of ski resorts as a winter destination, but they offer many fun activities in the summer as well. When our family stayed in Breckenridge, Colorado, last summer, we took a chair lift to a restaurant at the summit of one of the mountains. We snapped dozens of photographs of the mountain scenery and the bountiful wildflowers on the way up. On the deck of the restaurant, we ate a hearty lunch of delicious hamburgers and homemade French fries. The next day, we rode bicycles along a bike path that wound through beautiful fields and cool forests. The path was fairly flat, so the riding was quite enjoyable. Our best day, however, was the day we went horseback riding through lush green meadows with spectacular mountains in the distance. We all bought cowboy hats and enjoyed a little taste of the Wild West. Next summer, our family plans to travel to another ski resort.

a. Most people think of ski resorts as a winter destination, but they offer many fun activities in the summer as well.
b. We snapped dozens of photographs of the mountain scenery and the bountiful wildflowers on the way up.
c. On the deck of the restaurant, we ate a hearty lunch of delicious hamburgers and homemade French fries.
d. . We all bought cowboy hats and enjoyed a little taste of the Wild West.

3. Which of the following topics is narrow enough to be developed in a paragraph?
    a. Using cloth towels and napkins at home can help conserve the environment.
    b. There are many ways to conserve the environment.
    c. Families can do a lot to help conserve the environment.
    d. Everyone can do his or her part to help conserve the environment.

4. Which of the following topics is narrow enough to be developed in a paragraph?
    a. New York City has a tremendous variety of restaurants.
    b. Italian restaurants are common in New York City.
    c. My favorite place to eat in New York City is Tony's Bistro.
    d. I will always remember New York City for its many Italian restaurants.

5. Which of the following topics is too general to be developed in a paragraph?
    a. Choosing a career involves many considerations.
    b. For high traffic areas in a house, it's important to choose the right carpet.
    c. Making your own salsa is fun and easy.
    d. The best gift I ever received was a scrapbook from my mother.

6. Which of the following topic sentences includes a controlling idea?
    a. Myra has a dog that can perform some unusual tricks.
    b. Jackson works at the post office.
    c. Yesterday, we had a snowstorm.
    d. For his birthday, Derrick received a new wallet.

7. Which of the following topic sentences is the most effective?
    a. In this paragraph I will explain how to change the oil in a car.
    b. Cynthia's talent for photography has led to many prestigious awards.
    c. Reasons to own a house rather than rent.
    d. Exercise is good for one's health.

8. Which of the following topic sentences is the most effective?
    a. Ways to enjoy the holidays on a budget.
    b. Most people experience stress.
    c. This paragraph will focus on health care for the elderly.
    d. Toby and Jan's beach wedding was the most romantic one I have ever seen.

9. Which sentences below would NOT support the following topic sentence?
    My cousin Arthur has an odd style of dressing.

    a. He wears farmer style denim overalls to school.
    b. On most days, he wears purple tennis shoes.
    c. He is a member of the drama club at school.
    d. He wears only yellow t-shirts under his overalls.

10. Identify the topic sentence in the paragraph below:

Our master bathroom needs some major improvements. First, the floor tiles must be replaced. A plumbing leak a few years ago resulted in stained tile. We will probably hire a professional to replace the tiles. Also, the shower floor needs new tiles. Several of the tiles are cracked and are difficult to keep clean. In addition, we would like to replace the single sink with a double sink. Having two sinks will make it easier for my wife and me to get ready for work in the morning. Finally, we want to install better and more natural overhead lighting. The Hollywood lights currently over the mirror are dim and outdated. Now that we have determined the necessary improvements, we are anxious to get started on this project.

    a. Now that we have determined are anxious to get started on this project.
    b. Our master bathroom needs some major improvements.
    c. Several of the tiles are cracked and are difficult to keep clean.
    d. A plumbing leak a few years ago resulted in stained tile.

11. Which of the body sentences does NOT support the topic sentence?

Our master bathroom needs some major improvements. First, the floor tiles must be replaced. A plumbing leak a few years ago resulted in stained tile. We will probably hire a professional to replace the tiles. Also, the shower floor needs new tiles. Several of the tile are cracked and are difficult to keep clean. In addition, we would like to replace the single sink with a double sink. Having two sinks will make it easier for my wife and me to get ready for work in the morning. Finally, we want to install better and more natural overhead lighting. The Hollywood lights currently over the mirror are dim and outdated. Now that we have determined the necessary improvements, we are anxious to get started on this project.

    a. We will probably hire a professional to replace the tiles.
    b. Also, we would like to replace the single sink with a double sink.
    c. Finally, we want to install better and more natural overhead lighting.
    d. Also, the shower floor needs new tiles.

12. Which organizational pattern is used in the following paragraph?

Our master bathroom needs some major improvements. First, the floor tiles must be replaced. A plumbing leak a few years ago resulted in stained tile. We will probably hire a professional to replace the tiles. Also, the shower floor needs new tiles. Several of the tile are cracked and are difficult to keep clean. In addition, we would like to replace the single sink with a double sink. Having two sinks will make it easier for my wife and me to get ready for work in the morning. Finally, we want to install better and more natural overhead lighting. The Hollywood lights currently over the mirror are dim and outdated. Now that we have determined the necessary improvements, we are anxious to get started on this project.

    a. time order
    b. alphabetical order
    c. space order
    d. emphatic order

13. Which of the following supporting examples is out of order if you are writing about the most important reasons to begin an exercise program and are organizing your examples in emphatic order?
    a. Aerobic exercise three or four days a week will improve cardiac health.
    b. Aerobic exercise will improve muscle tone.
    c. Aerobic exercise will reduce stress and stress-related ailments.
    d. Aerobic exercise will provide more energy for work and play.

14. If you are describing the new home that you just bought, you would most likely use
    a. time order.
    b. alphabetical order.
    c. emphatic order.
    d. space order.

15. If you are writing a story about how your car ended up in the impound lot, you would most likely use
    a. time order.
    b. alphabetical order.
    c. emphatic order.
    d. space order.

The Writer's World: Sentences and Paragraphs, 3rd Edition
CHAPTER 3: REVISING AND EDITING

Summary

Chapter 3: Revising and Editing discusses revising for unity, adequate support, coherence, and style as well as editing for errors in the final draft.

Unity is explained as ensuring that all sentences support the topic sentence. An example of a paragraph without unity is presented. Practice 1 asks students to read three paragraphs and to remove any sentence that violates unity.

Revising for adequate support is explained as ensuring that paragraphs contain strong and convincing supporting details. An edited example is presented for review. In Practice 2, students add details for supporting examples in an exercise paragraph. A hint box cautions students to avoid circular reasoning. In Practice 3, students supply supporting examples for three short passages.

The section on revising for coherences introduces the use of transitional expressions. A list of common transitional expressions and their meanings is provided. In a hint box, students are advised to check for complete sentences with transitions. In Practice 4, students add transitional expressions to a paragraph.

Revising for style is explained as varying sentence structure, using exact language, and avoiding repetitious or vague language. An example paragraph containing revised style errors is presented.

The next section of this chapter, editing for errors, instructs students to look for mistakes in grammar, punctuation, mechanics, and spelling. A hint box suggests putting aside work for a day or two before editing and also to keep a spelling and grammar log. An example of an edited paragraph is presented.

The Writer's Desk instructs students to choose a paragraph written for Chapter 2 or for another assignment and to revise and edit it. Peer feedback is briefly discussed, and a hint box provides suggestions about how to phrase criticism positively. A peer feedback form is provided.

The last section of this chapter focuses on the final draft. The Writer's Desk instructs students to write the final draft and then proofread it before handing it in. In The Writer's Room, Activity 1, asks students to choose a paragraph that they have written for this course, then revise, edit, and write the final draft. Writing Activity 2 instructs students to choose one of ten topics provided and write a paragraph. The revising and editing checklist advises students to ask themselves whether their paragraph has unity, adequate support, coherence, and effective style. The checklist also reminds students to check for errors in grammar, punctuation, spelling, and mechanics.

At chapter's end, students are referred to MyWritingLabfor additional practice.

Set 1: Testing Concepts

1. When you revise your writing, you
   a. organize your writing by making a paragraph plan.
   b. narrow your topic.
   c. modify your writing to make it more convincing and precise.
   d. proofread your final draft for errors in grammar, spelling, punctuation, and mechanics.

2. When you edit your writing, you
   a. organize your writing by making a paragraph plan.
   b. narrow your topic.
   c. modify your writing to make it more convincing and precise.
   d. proofread your final draft for errors in grammar, spelling, punctuation, and mechanics.

3. When you revise for adequate support, you
   a. make sure that your sentences are varied and interesting.
   b. make sure that all parts of your work relate to the main idea.
   c. ensure that you have enough details to effectively support the main idea.
   d. verify that your ideas flow smoothly and are logically linked.

4. When you revise for unity, you
   a. make sure that your sentences are varied and interesting.
   b. make sure that all parts of your work relate to the main idea.
   c. ensure that you have enough details to effectively support the main idea.
   d. verify that your ideas flow smoothly and are logically linked.

5. When you revise for style, you
   a. verify that your ideas flow smoothly and are logically linked.
   b. make sure that your sentences are varied and interesting.
   c. proofread your work and correct errors in grammar, punctuation, and mechanics.
   d. make sure that all parts of your work relate to the main idea.

6. When you revise for coherence, you
   a. verify that your ideas flow smoothly and are logically linked.
   b. proofread your work and correct errors in grammar, punctuation, and mechanics.
   c. make sure that all parts of your work relate to the main idea.
   d. make sure that your sentences are varied and interesting.

7. Circular reasoning occurs when
     a. the writer presents only one example to support a point.
     b. the writer refers to earlier examples in the paragraph or essay.
     c. the writer restates the main point in various ways but does not provide supporting details.
     d. the writer presents supporting examples and details that are not arranged in a logical order.

8. When you edit for technical errors, you
     a. verify that your ideas flow smoothly and are logically linked.
     b. make sure that your sentences are varied and interesting.
     c. proofread your work and correct errors in grammar, punctuation, and mechanics.
     d. make sure that all parts of your work relate to the main idea.

9. All of the following are common transitional expressions except
     a. in addition.
     b. on the other hand.
     c. for example.
     d. and.

10. You can achieve coherence in your paragraph by using
     a. transitional expressions.
     b. effective prepositions.
     c. vivid descriptive details.
     d. a clear topic sentence.

11. You can improve your writing style by
     a. creating a strong topic sentence.
     b. varying your sentence structure and using concise wording.
     c. using very formal, sophisticated language.
     d. using casual language and slang.

12. When you edit your work, it is a good idea to
     a. put your work aside for a day or two before you edit it.
     b. edit your work in every step of the writing process.
     c. edit your work right after you finish the first draft.
     d. begin editing your work in the exploration step of writing.

13. You should turn in your final draft
     a. after your revise it.
     b. after you revise it and after you proofread it for errors in grammar, punctuation, spelling, and mechanics.
     c. as soon as you finish it.
     d. at least two days late so that your instructor knows how hard you worked on it.

14. Peer feedback means
   a. asking a friend or fellow student to read your work and provide suggestions.
   b. asking a friend or fellow student to revise your work for you.
   c. using a computer's grammar and spell checker programs to edit your work.
   d. putting your work aside for a few days before you revise or edit it.

15. When you make suggestions for a fellow student's writing, your comments should be
   a. vague.
   b. somewhat untruthful to avoid hurting anyone's feelings.
   c. blunt but honest.
   d. constructive and helpful.

Set 2: Testing Applications

1. Identify the topic sentence in the passage below:
   The hotel we chose for our weekend stay in Dallas was a poor one. We were in town for a business meeting. The rooms were dark and dingy, and both bedspreads were torn. In addition, there was an iron-shaped hole burned in the carpet. The breakfast room in the lobby was even worse than the dreary room. The waffle maker was heavily crusted with old batter. The orange juice dispenser delivered pale, watery orange juice, and the coffee was weak. Finally, the bread was so stale that the corners were curled upward. We should have read the online reviews before we made our reservations.
   a. The hotel we chose for our weekend stay in Dallas was a poor one.
   b. We were in town for a business meeting.
   c. The breakfast room in the lobby was even worse than the dreary room.
   d. The waffle maker was heavily crusted with old batter.

2. Which sentence in the paragraph below should be deleted to maintain paragraph unity?
   The hotel we chose for our weekend stay in Dallas was a poor one. We were in town for a business meeting. The rooms were dark and dingy, and both bedspreads were torn. In addition, there was an iron-shaped hole burned in the carpet. The breakfast room in the lobby was even worse than the dreary room. The waffle maker was heavily crusted with old batter. The orange juice dispenser delivered pale, watery orange juice, and the coffee was weak. Finally, the bread was so stale that the corners were curled upward. We should have read the online reviews before we made our reservations.
   a. The hotel we chose for our weekend stay in Dallas was a poor one.
   b. We were in town for a business meeting.
   c. The breakfast room in the lobby was even worse than the dreary room.
   d. The waffle maker was heavily crusted with old batter.

3. Which transition, if inserted between the two sentences below, will provide greater coherence between the two ideas?
   The waffle maker was heavily crusted with old batter. _____, the orange juice dispenser delivered pale, watery orange juice, and the coffee was weak.
   a. nevertheless
   b. for example
   c. also
   d. however

4. Identify the topic sentence in the paragraph below:

Megan loves her new smartphone. She can send text messages easily. She can send pictures and even videos attached to her text messages. Megan also appreciates being able to check and answer her email from her phone. Her favorite feature, however, is the GPS system. It allows her to find her way around large cities quite easily. Megan said that she cannot imagine going back to her old cell phone.

    a. Megan loves her new smartphone.
    b. She can send text messages easily.
    c. Her favorite feature, however, is the GPS system.
    d. It allows her to find her way around large cities quite easily.

5. Which sentence, if inserted into the paragraph below, would disrupt the unity of the paragraph?

Megan loves her new smartphone. She can send text messages easily. She can send pictures and even videos attached to her text messages. Megan also appreciates being able to check and answer her email from her phone. Her favorite feature, however, is the GPS system. It allows her to find her way around large cities quite easily. Megan said that she cannot imagine going back to her old cell phone.

    a Yesterday she sent a picture of her new niece to her best friend in Italy.
    b. She used her phone's GPS to find a French bakery in downtown Dallas.
    c. Megan also has a new iPod, which she loves.
    d. For example, she answered an urgent email from her boss about her schedule.

6. Which transition, if inserted between the sentences below, would provide stronger coherence between the two ideas?

She can send text messages easily. _____, she can send pictures and even videos attached to her text messages

    a. however
    b. for example
    c. on the other hand
    d. in addition

7. What is the most obvious weakness in the following paragraph?

The pizza crust is thick but not tough, and the sauce is tangy with just a hint of garlic. Also, the vegetables are fresh and tasty. The onions are crisp, not wilted; furthermore, the mushrooms are fresh, not canned. Finally, Clair is generous with the cheese; she uses a blend of three different cheeses. Her pizzas smell like wonderful European cheeses when she when she pulls them out of the oven. She can invite me to her place anytime for her homemade pizza.

    a. The paragraph has no topic sentence.
    b. The paragraph does not have adequate supporting examples.
    c. The paragraph lacks transitions.
    d. The paragraph lacks unity.

8. Choose the sentence that most effectively supports the topic sentence below:

Yesterday, the weather was miserable.

    a. It was raining.

b. The wind was blowing hard.

c. It was also very cold.

d. It rained over three inches, and an icy wind seemed to blow right through my jacket.

9. Choose the sentence that most effectively supports the topic sentence below:

My new car has some great features.

a. The car came with modern, up-to-date technology as standard features.

b. The car has a GPS mapping system as well as a back-up camera.

c. I especially like the technical gadgets that came with the car.

d. The passenger's seats, as well as the driver's seat, are adjustable.

10. Choose the sentence that most effectively supports the topic sentence below:

Lori eats very healthful breakfasts.

a. She eats fresh fruits and some type of whole wheat bread.

b. She adds protein to her fruit smoothies, which are made from fresh fruits.

c. She also eats a small handful of raw nuts daily as well as fresh fruits.

d. She adds protein powder to her fresh raspberry and banana smoothie every morning.

11. Which of the following transitions establishes the most effective coherence between the two sentences below?

The brochure promised a stunning view of the ocean; _____ , we had a view of the parking lot.

a. consequently

b. nevertheless

c. instead

d. for example

12. Which of the following transitions establishes the most effective coherence between the two sentences below?

Jon began eating salads for dinner instead of fast foods; _____ , he lost three pounds this week.

a. however

b. as a result

c. for instance

d. furthermore

13. Which of the sentences below demonstrates the clearest and most concise language?

a. Jewel's performance at the concert was amazing.

b. The meal that we had at the steak house was wonderful.

c. Yesterday's staff meeting was a waste of time.

d. Kevin loves all creatures so much that he won't even kill a spider.

14. Which of the sentences below demonstrates the clearest and most concise language?

a. My cat isn't hungry; she turned her nose up at fresh tuna fish.

b. The view from our restaurant window was awesome.

c. Martin's speech was incredible.
d. Lunch is served with a variety of beverages.

15. Which of the passages below demonstrates the clearest and most concise language?
    a. Jenny grows beautiful flowers in her back yard.
    b. Bentley's dog can do some very cool tricks.
    c. Oak trees were silhouetted against the pale orange sunset.
    d. We stopped alongside the road to admire a beautiful meadow.

The Writer's World: Sentences and Paragraphs, 3ʳᵈ Edition
CHAPTER 4: PARAGRAPH PATTERNS
Summary

Chapter 4: Paragraph Patterns introduces nine rhetorical modes, the methods writers use to develop a piece of writing. All nine modes, from illustration to argument, are listed and each is followed by a brief description of its purpose.

A thorough discussion of each of the paragraph patterns—illustration, narration, description, process, definition, comparison and contrast, cause and effect, classification, and argument—is presented.

For each lesson, an example paragraph is featured, followed by a practice exercise that asks students to identify key parts of the paragraph. Writer's Desk exercises take students through each step of the writing process for each pattern: exploring, developing, organizing, drafting, and revision and editing.

At the end of each paragraph pattern, The Writer's Room, Activity 1, asks students to choose a topic from several subjects listed and write a paragraph using the specified pattern. Activity 2 asks students to look at a photograph to generate an idea for a paragraph. Each section ends with a checklist for the specific paragraph pattern.

At chapter's end, students are directed to MyWritingLab for further review.

Set 1: Testing Concepts

1. The method writers can use to develop a piece of writing is called
   a. revision.
   b. editing.
   c. individual style.
   d. patterns or modes.

2. When you write an illustration paragraph, you
   a. explain why an event happened or the consequences of the event.
   b. prove your point using specific examples.
   c. tell a story about something that happened.
   d. present information about similarities or differences.

3. If you write a narrative paragraph, you might
   a. tell a story about something that happened.
   b. define or explain a term.
   c. explain how to do something or how something works.
   d. describe a person or a place.

4. When you write a description paragraph, you
   a. take a position on an issue and offer reasons for your position.
   b. describe a place or person using vivid details and images.
   c. explain how to do something or how something works.
   d. define or explain a term.

5. When you write a definition paragraph, you
   a. define or explain a term.
   b. present information about similarities or differences.
   c. prove your point by using specific examples.
   d. take a position on an issue and offer reasons for your position.

6. When you write a process paragraph, you
   a. explain why an event happened or what the consequences of the event were.
   b. take a position on an issue and offer reasons for your position.
   c. explain how to do something or how something works.
   d. tell a story about something that happened.

7. When you write a cause and effect paragraph, you
    a. explain how to do something or how something works.
    b. take a position on an issue and offer reasons for your position.
    c. tell a story about something that happened.
    d. explain why an event happened or what the consequences of that event were.

8. When you write a comparison or contrast paragraph, you
    a. define or explain a term.
    b. present information about similarities or differences.
    c. prove your point by using specific examples.
    d. take a position on an issue and offer reasons for your position.

9. The topic sentence of a paragraph consists of the topic and
    a. at least one supporting detail.
    b. transitions.
    c. a controlling idea.
    d. all the supporting details.

10. When you write an argument paragraph, you
    a. take a position on an issue and offer reasons for your position.
    b. explain how to do something or how something works.
    c. tell a story about something that happened.
    d. explain why an event happened or what the consequences of that event were.

11. The two main kinds of narrative writing are
    a. second person and third person.
    b. second person and present tense.
    c. first person and second person.
    d. first person and third person.

12. The supporting ideas in a paragraph
    a. should be general, not specific.
    b. support the topic sentence.
    c. establish the direction of the paragraph.
    d. all of the above

13. In an argument paragraph, the topic sentence mentions the subject and
    a. a universal truth.
    b. a supporting detail.
    c. a dominant impression.
    d. a debatable point.

14. When you establish the dominant impression in a descriptive paragraph, you
  a. use generalizations.
  b. convey a specific overall mood.
  c. convey the supporting details.
  d. establish a persuasive point.

15. The organizational pattern for a process paragraph is
  a. emphatic order.
  b. random order.
  c. time order.
  d. space order.

Set 2: Testing Applications

1. Which of the following topics is most suitable for an illustration pattern of development?
    a. ways to eat healthfully on a budget
    b. how tornadoes are formed
    c. an argument against school uniforms
    d. how I managed to break my favorite serving bowl

2. Which of the following topics is most suitable for a narration paragraph?
    a. why Marge's homemade bread is always tough
    b. my first speeding ticket
    c. reasons thatJack quit his job
    d. how to change a flat tire

3. Which of the following topics is most suitable for a descriptive paragraph?
    a. the damage done to the vegetable garden by pests
    b. how to get on a moving ski lift
    c. ways to improve sales
    d. an argument to ban smoking at outdoor events

4. Which of the following topics is most suitable for a process paragraph?
    a. the suspected causes of the bridge collapse
    b. what it means to be honest
    c. the benefits of daily meditation
    d. how to plant an herb garden

5. Which of the following topics is most suitable for a comparison or contrast paragraph?
    a. a car accident that I witnessed
    b. how Professor White's tests differ from Professor Anderson's
    c. ways to study effectively
    d. reasons thatPaula needs a new car

6. Which of the following topics is most suitable for a cause or effect paragraph?
    a. reasons that Ted is the best supervisor in the company
    b. how the new software tracks client orders
    c. what will happen to our city's economy if Jones is elected as mayor
    d. the first time Lou went water skiing

7. Which of the following topics is most suitable for a definition paragraph?
    a. why Blake's latest novel is his best
    b. the meaning of responsibility
    c. ways to cut calories in fast food restaurants
    d. how to record shows on a DVD player

8. Which of the following topics is most suitable for an argument paragraph?
      a. the differences between Coach Williams and Coach Adams
      b. why Dave is driving a new red sports car
      c. why we should go to year-round schools
      d. how Kevin managed to fail his driving test

9. Identify the writing pattern of the paragraph below:
      Becoming a vegetarian has given me much more energy than I had before. When I was eating beef, pork, and chicken, I usually felt sluggish all day. In fact, in the afternoons, I felt so sleepy that I often had to take a nap. After I eliminated meat from my diet, I began waking up refreshed and staying alert all day long. I have the energy to exercise more often and for longer periods of time. Furthermore, I haven't needed an afternoon nap since I became a vegetarian.
      a. definition
      b. narration
      c. comparison and contrast
      d. process

10. Identify the topic sentence of the paragraph below:
      Becoming a vegetarian has given me much more energy than I had before. When I was eating beef, pork, and chicken, I usually felt sluggish all day. In fact, in the afternoons, I felt so sleepy that I often had to take a nap. After I eliminated meat from my diet, I began waking up refreshed and staying alert all day long. I have the energy to exercise more often and for longer periods of time. Furthermore, I haven't needed an afternoon nap since I became a vegetarian.
a. Furthermore, I haven't needed an afternoon nap since I became a vegetarian.
      b. After I eliminated meat from my diet, I began waking up refreshed and staying alert all day long.
      c. When I was eating beef, pork, and chicken, I usually felt sluggish all day.
      d. Becoming a vegetarian has given me much more energy than I had before.

11. What is the controlling idea of the following paragraph?
      a. I often felt so sleepy that I had to take an afternoon nap.
      b. Vegetarianism has given me more energy.
      c. I exercise more now than I did before.
      d. Eating meat used to make me feel sluggish.

12. Which of the following topics is most suitable for a cause or effect paragraph?
      a. how the aftermath of Hurricane Katrina affected us
      b. how we made our own holiday gifts from supplies around the house
      c. the difference between a mountain bike and a hybrid bike
      d. reasons that we should visit Aunt Sabrina soon

13. Which of the following topics is most suitable for a narration paragraph?
     a. how to put out a fire on the kitchen stove
     b. the major causes of last night's power failure
     c. the day Randall flew an airplane solo
     d. the meaning of friendship

14. Which of the following topics is most suitable for an argument paragraph?
     a. the qualities of an effective senator
     b. why jet skis on the lake should be banned
     c. the condition of the office furniture in the Toledo office
     d. why Justin has decided to accept a job in Seattle

15. Which of the following topics is most suitable for definition paragraph?
     a. what it means to be a compassionate person
     b. how the speed bumps have impacted the accident rate
     c. reasons that the remodeling of our house has taken so long
     d. how one detective solved a major cold case

Chapter 5: Writing the Essay moves from writing the paragraph to writing an essay. All steps of writing the essay are covered, from exploring through the final draft.

An essay is described as series of paragraphs that support one central idea, divided into an introduction, body, and a conclusion. The difference among a sentence, paragraph, and essay is explained, and examples are provided. The structure of an essay is explained, and a sample essay is provided with the various parts labeled and explained.

Exploring and narrowing the topic is discussed, and a student example is provided. In The Writer's Desk, students practice narrowing topics from broad subjects.

The section on developing ideas within an essay begins with an explanation of the thesis statement and characteristics of a good thesis statement: it expresses the main topic of the essay, it contains the controlling idea, and it is a complete sentence that usually appears in the introductory paragraph. Examples of effective and ineffective thesis statements are provided. A hint box reminds students to ensure that their thesis statement is clear and specific. In Practice 1, students review five faulty thesis statements and identify their specific faults. In The Writer's Desk, students practice writing thesis statements by choosing narrowed topics from the previous exercise.

The supporting ideas section begins with a diagram depicting the structure of an essay with supporting ideas, followed by a student example. In The Writer's Desk, students choose a thesis statement from the previous Writer's Desk exercise and create a list of supporting ideas.

The essay plan explains how to create an outline for an essay, and a student example is provided. In The Writer's Desk, students write an essay plan using their thesis statement and supporting details from the previous Writer's Desk exercise.

The introduction is next described, with a discussion of various methods to get the reader's attention. A hint box advises students that the thesis statement is generally the last sentence in the introduction. In Practice 2, students read three introductory paragraphs and then identify the introduction style being used.

The conclusion is explained as a paragraph that rephrases the thesis and summarizes the main points in the essay. A student example is presented, and a hint box cautions students against contradicting their main point or introducing new or irrelevant information. In Practice 3, students write an introductory paragraph for an essay. In The Writer's Desk, students write an introduction and conclusion for the essay plan they created for a previous exercise.

The next section discusses the first draft, and The Writer's Desk asks students to create a first draft based on the essay plan created in the previous exercise.

Revising and editing is then discussed in depth, with an emphasis on revising for unity, adequate support, and coherence, then editing for errors. In The Writer's Desk, students revise and edit the essay they wrote for the previous Writer's Desk exercise.

For the final draft, students write and proofread the final draft of their essay for submission to the instructor. In The Writer's Room, Activity 1, students choose a topic from ten ideas and write an essay. In Writing Activity 2, students write an essay based on a photograph.

The essay checklist reminds students to ensure that they have considered exploring, developing, and revising and editing. At chapter's end, students are directed to MyWritingLab for further study.

Set 1: Testing Concepts

1. An essay is
   a. a series of paragraphs that are about one central idea.
   b. a sentence that contains a thesis and a controlling idea.
   c. a series of sentences that support a topic sentence.
   d. any written material that includes documented research.

2. An essay consists of
   a. an introduction and documented research.
   b. one body paragraph, a thesis statement, and a conclusion.
   c. an introduction, body, and conclusion.
   d. a topic sentence, supporting details, and transitions.

3. The introduction of an essay engages the reader's interest and
   a. contains supporting examples and details.
   b. contains the topic sentence.
   c. contains the thesis statement.
   d. all of the above

4. Body paragraphs provide
   a. the conclusion.
   b. support for the thesis.
   c. the thesis statement.
   d. the topic sentence.

5. When you narrow the topic for an essay, you
   a. make the topic more specific.
   b. ensure that you use only one supporting example.
   c. expand the scope of the topic.
   d. all of the above

6. What is the perfect length for an essay?
   a. All essays should contain just five paragraphs.
   b. All essays should contain at least 500 words.
   c. All essays should be at least two pages in length.
   d. There is no perfect length for an essay.

7. The thesis statement
   a. establishes the mood of the essay.
   b. establishes and makes a point about the topic of an essay.
   c. establishes the topic of a paragraph.
   d. establishes the supporting examples in a paragraph.

8. An effective thesis statement should
   a. be a complete sentence that usually appears in the essay's introductory paragraph.
   b. express the main topic of the essay.
   c. contain a controlling idea.
   d. all of the above

9. To write an essay plan, you should do all of the following except
   a. edit your work carefully for errors in grammar, punctuation, spelling, and mechanics.
   b. add details under each topic sentence.
   c. look at your list of ideas and identify the best supporting ideas.
   d. write topic sentences that express the main supporting ideas.

10. To generate ideas for body paragraphs, you could
    a. search the Internet for a sample essay.
    b. begin writing the first draft immediately.
    c. use exploring ideas such as brainstorming, clustering, or freewriting.
    d. make an outline.

11. The conclusion of an essay
    a. contains details that support the body paragraphs.
    b. rephrases the thesis statement.
    c. summarizes the main points in the essay.
    d. both b and c

12. When you revise your essay, you
    a. write an organizational plan for your essay.
    b. establish a clear, strong thesis.
    c. improve faulty logic, poor organization, or poor sentence style.
    d. proofread your essay for errors in grammar, punctuation, spelling, and mechanics.

13. When you edit your essay, you
    a. proofread your essay for errors in grammar, punctuation, spelling, and mechanics.
    b. ensure that all details and examples are supporting the thesis statement.
    c. ensure that there are enough details and examples to make your essay strong and convincing.
    d. ensure that your paragraphs flow smoothly and are logically organized.

14. An effective introductory paragraph contains the thesis statement and
    a. captures the reader's attention.
    b. contains all the examples that support the thesis.
    c. makes an announcement about what you intend to show in the essay.
    d. none of the above

15. When you revise for unity, you
    a. proofread your essay for errors in grammar, punctuation, spelling, and mechanics.
    b. ensure that all details and examples are supporting the thesis statement.
    c. ensure that there are enough details and examples to make your essay strong and convincing.
    d. ensure that your paragraphs flow smoothly and are logically organized.

Set 2: Testing Applications

1. Which of the following statements would be an effective thesis statement?
   a. Rain is good for the land.
   b. This essay will list ways to budget for the holidays.
   c. Places to visit in San Diego.
   d. The Benson family has a unique way to celebrate birthdays.

2. Which of the following statements would be an effective thesis statement?
   a. Teachers assign too much homework.
   b. A minor car accident taught me about the kindness of strangers.
   c. In this essay, I will discuss ways to have a successful garage sale.
   d. Carl lives on Brooks Street, near the lake.

3. Identify the problem with the following thesis statement:
   Trish, a woman who needs no introduction.
   a. The thesis is too narrow.
   b. The thesis is too broad and is common knowledge.
   c. The thesis makes an announcement.
   d. The thesis is an incomplete sentence.

4. Identify the problem with the following thesis statement:
   Good health is important for everyone.
   a. The thesis is too narrow.
   b. The thesis is too broad.
   c. The thesis makes an announcement.
   d. The thesis is an incomplete sentence.

5. Identify the problem with the following thesis statement:
   Luke received a credit card application in the mail.
   a. The thesis makes an announcement.
   b. The thesis is too narrow.
   c. The thesis is worded vaguely.
   d. The thesis makes an invalid point.

6. Which of the following thesis statements is sufficiently narrow?
   a. There are many things to do in Orlando, Florida.
   b. College sports programs provide many benefits to athletes.
   c. NASA's space program has a long and interesting history.
   d. Making homemade power bars is inexpensive and easy.

7. Which of the following thesis statements is sufficiently narrow?
   a. Selling unwanted items on eBay is a good way to earn extra money.
   b. The mall offers a wide variety of stores and restaurants.
   c. There are many different varieties of flowers.
   d. Exercise is good for one's health.

8. Which of the following thesis statements is sufficiently broad?
   a. Norman was born in Boise, Idaho, in 1989.
   b. The Columbia River divides Oregon from Washington.
   c. My new cell phone has some very useful features.
   d. Danielle's cat weighs twelve pounds.

9. Identify the introduction style used in the introductory paragraph below:
   "To thine own self be true," Polonius told Laertes in Hamlet. *Those words are as true and wise today as they were when Shakespeare wrote them.*
   a. interesting anecdote
   b. quotation
   c. historical
   d. opposite position

10. Identify the introduction style used in the introductory paragraph below:
   Native Americans once stood on rocks and wooden platforms on the banks of Celilo Falls, Oregon, on the Columbia River, and fished for salmon. In 1957 these beautiful falls were permanently flooded when The Dalles Dam was built. Today the Hood River Valley has plenty of power, and The Dalles Dam has provided many jobs. Celilo Falls, which means "echo of falling water," has been silenced forever. We have paid a dear price for power.
   a. anecdotal
   b. general
   c. historical
   d. opposite position

11. Identify the thesis statement in the introductory paragraph below:
   Native Americans once stood on rocks and wooden platforms on the banks of Celilo Falls, Oregon, on the Columbia River, and fished for salmon. In 1957 these beautiful falls were permanently flooded when The Dalles Dam was built. Today the Hood River Valley has plenty of power, and The Dalles Dam has provided many jobs. Celilo Falls, which means "echo of falling water," has been silenced forever. We have paid a dear price for power.
   a. Native Americans once stood on rocks and wooden platforms on the banks of Celilo Falls, Oregon, on the Columbia River, and fished for salmon.
   b. In 1957 these beautiful falls were permanently flooded when The Dalles Dam was built.
   c. Today the Hood River Valley has plenty of power, and The Dalles Dam has provided many jobs.
   d. We have paid a dear price for power.

12. Which of the following statements would be an effective thesis statement?
   a. Yosemite National Park, a place of discovery and beauty.
   b. This essay will discuss ways to handle a job interview successfully.
   c. Reality TV shows are very popular.
   d. Getting more sleep at night can actually help you lose weight.

13. Which of the following statements would be an effective thesis statement?
   a. Handing over your credit card in a restaurant can easily result in identity theft.
   b. A hurricane struck the Gulf Coast of Florida recently.
   c. Alaska, the last frontier of wilderness.
   d. This essay will explain how to make homemade granola.

14. Identify the conclusion style used in the conclusion below:
   The television robs us of time, time to finish chores, time to talk to family members, even time to spend with our own thoughts. Try shutting off the television for just a weekend and see what a difference the silence makes.
   a. a prediction
   b. a suggestion
   c. a quotation
   d. an anecdote

15. Identify the conclusion style used in the conclusion below:
   As fast food restaurants continue to spring up on nearly every corner, our temptation to grab a quick meal increases. The more we give in to such convenience, the more our health will suffer.
   a. a prediction
   b. a suggestion
   c. a quotation
   d. an anecdote

Chapter 6: Nouns, Determiners, and Prepositions begins with a Grammar Snapshot paragraph that demonstrates the use of nouns, determiners, and prepositions. Nouns are defined and categorized as common, proper, singular, and plural. Special note is made of irregular plural nouns. A hint box explains that –es is added to the plural form of nouns ending in –s. A list of spellings of singular and plural nouns is provided. A hint box explains the two plural forms of people: *persons* and *people*.

In Practice 1, students fill in the blank with singular and plural forms of nouns for fifteen nouns. In Practice 2, students correct an incorrect plural noun form in eight sentences. A hint box explains key words indicating singular and plural nouns. In Practice 3, students underline key words in eight sentences that help determine whether nouns are singular or plural and then correct errors in singular and plural nouns. A hint box explains the use of plural nouns after *of the* expressions. In Practice 4, students correct ten errors with singular and plural nouns found in three passages.

Count and Noncount nouns are then defined and discussed. A list of examples is provided. In Practice 5, students change nouns to plural forms in ten sentences.

Determiners are defined as words that identify whether a noun is specific or general. Examples are provided, and a hint box advises students to use *a* before words beginning with a consonant and *an* before words that begin with vowels. Another hint box cautions students to avoid overusing *the*. In Practice 6, students write the correct article before the noun in three short passages.

Special attention is given to the pronouns *many, few, much, little, this, that, these,* and *those*. In Practice 7, students choose the best determiners in three short passages. In Practice 8, Review, students correct twelve errors with singular nouns, plural nouns, and determiners in two passages.

Prepositions are defined as words that show concepts such as time, place, direction, and manner. Emphasis is given to prepositions expressing time and place. A chart is presented, and a hint box discusses the difference between *to* and *at*. In Practice 9, students choose the correct prepositions in ten sentences. Another hint box discusses the differences among *for, during,* and *since*. Practice 10 asks students to correct six errors with prepositions in a short passage.

Common prepositional expressions are discussed next, and a chart illustrates the most common expressions. In Practice 11, students fill in the correct prepositions in three passages.

In the Final Review, students correct errors in singular and plural nouns and determiners found in three passages. In The Writer's Room, students choose one of two topics listed and write about it, identifying plural nouns and determiners. The checklist reminds students to use the correct singular and plural forms of nouns, to use the correct determiners, and to use the correct prepositions.

At chapter's end, students are directed to MyWritingLab for further review.

CHAPTER 6: NOUNS, DETERMINERS, AND PREPOSITIONS
Exercises

Set 1: Testing Concepts

1. A noun
    a. describes something.
    b. refers to people, places, or things.
    c. expresses action.
    d. all of the above

2. A proper noun refers to
    a. things, but not people or places.
    b. people, but not things or places.
    c. general people, places, or things and begins with a lowercase letter.
    d. particular people, places, or things and begins with a capital letter.

3. A common noun refers to
    a. physical action.
    b. mental action.
    c. general people, places, or things and begins with a lowercase letter.
    d. particular people, places, or things and begins with a capital letter.

4. Nouns can be
    a. singular.
    b. plural.
    c. irregular.
    d. all of the above

5. To form the plural of most nouns ending in –*f* or –*fe*, such as *calf,*
    a. change the –*f* to –*v* and add –*es*.
    b. change the –*f* to –*ie* and add –*s*.
    c. add –*es*.
    d. add –*s*.

6. To form the plural of nouns ending in a consonant + –*y*, such as *ruby,*
    a. add –*es*.
    b. add –*s*.
    c. change the –*y* to –*i* and add –*es*.
    d. change –*y* to –*e* and add –*s*.

7. After words such as *a, an, one, each, every,* and *another*, use
    a. only a common noun.
    b. only a proper noun.
    c. a plural noun.
    d. a singular noun.

8. To form the plural of nouns ending in a vowel + -*y*, such as *ray*,
    a. add –*es*.
    b. add –*s*.
    c. change the –*y* to –*i* and add –*es*.
    d. change –*y* to –*e* and add –*vs*.

9. *Of the* expressions are followed by
    a. only a common noun.
    b. only a proper noun.
    c. a plural noun.
    d. a singular noun.

10. After words such as *two, all, both, many, few, several,* and *some,* use
    a. only a common noun.
    b. only a proper noun.
    c. a plural noun.
    d. a singular noun.

11. A *count noun* refers to
    a. all common nouns.
    b. all proper nouns.
    c. things that cannot be counted because they cannot be divided.
    d. things that can be counted.

12. A *noncount* noun refers to
    a. things that cannot be counted because they cannot be divided.
    b. things that can be counted.
    c. all common nouns.
    d. all proper nouns.

13. A word that identifies or determines if a noun is specific or general is called
    a. a determiner.
    b. a pronoun.
    c. a count noun.
    d. a noncount noun.

14. All of the following words are prepositions except
   a. from.
   b. in.
   c. when.
   d. by.

15. Words that show concepts of time, place, direction, and manner are called
   a. determiners.
   b. prepositions.
   c. nouns.
   d. pronouns.

Set 2: Testing Applications

1. Choose the plural word below that is spelled incorrectly.
   a. moose
   b. knives
   c. shelfs
   d. lives

2. Choose the plural noun below that is spelled incorrectly.
   a. babies
   b. wolves
   c. berries
   d. sheeps

3. Choose the plural noun below that is spelled incorrectly.
   a. tooths
   b. children
   c. factories
   d. themselves

4. Choose the plural noun below that is spelled incorrectly.
   a. familys
   b. deer
   c. babies
   d. ladies

5. Choose the correctly spelled word for the blank in the sentence below:
   At night, we could hear several _____ howling.
   a. wolfs
   b. wolves
   c. wolfs'
   d. wolfes

6. Choose the correctly spelled word for the blank in the sentence below:
   As the airplane descended, I could hear a few _____ crying.
   a. babys
   b. baby's
   c. babyes
   d. babies

7. Choose the correctly spelled word for the blank in the sentence below:
   Several _____ were taking pictures of the bear cubs.
   a. tourist
   b. touristes
   c. tourists
   d. tourist's

8. Choose the correctly spelled word for the blank in the sentence below:

Most of the _____ in my kitchen are quite dull.

   a. knives
   b. knifes
   c. knivs
   d. knifs

9. Choose the correctly spelled word for the blank in the sentence below:

You must all act like true _____ and gentlemen this evening.

   a. ladys
   b. ladies
   c. ladeys
   d. lady's

10. Choose the correctly spelled word for the blank in the sentence below:

Little Abby has two new _____.

   a. tooths
   b. teeths
   c. toothes
   d. teeth

11. Choose the correct form of the noun for the blank in the sentence below:

Dozens of _____ studied the latest volcanic eruption.

   a. scientist
   b. scientists
   c. scientist's
   d. scientistes

12. Choose the correct form of the noun for the blank in the sentence below:

Two of the _____ on our street already have their holiday lights up.

   a. families
   b. familys
   c. familyies
   d. family's

13. Choose the correct form of the noun for the blank in the sentence below:

Chan's new job is in _____.

   a. a hospital.
   b. an hospital.
   c. this hospitals.
   d. a hospitals.

14. Choose the correct preposition for the blank in the sentence below:
     I can't go to Starbucks with you because I have to go _____.
     a. in the work.
     b. at work.
     c. to work.
     d. in work.

15. Choose the correct preposition for the blank in the sentence below:
     A small dog followed me _____ yesterday.
     a. to home
     b. in home
     c. on home
     d. home

The Writer's World: Sentences and Paragraphs, 3rd Edition
CHAPTER 7: PRONOUNS
Summary

  Chapter 7: Pronouns covers pronoun-antecedent agreement, indefinite pronouns, vague pronouns, pronoun shifts, pronoun case, problems with possessive pronouns, relative pronouns, and reflexive pronouns.

  The chapter opens with a Grammar Snapshot, a paragraph excerpt with all pronouns underlined.

  Antecedents are defined, and a hint box discusses compound antecedents, those joined by *and* and those joined by *or*. In Practice 1, students identify antecedents in eight sentences. A hint box explains collective nouns. In Practice 2, students identify the antecedent and fill in the correct pronoun in seven sentences.

  Indefinite pronouns are defined, and a list of singular, plural, and either singular or plural pronouns is presented. Examples of each in sentences are also presented. A hint box reminds students how to locate the subject in *of the* expressions. In Practice 3, students identify the correct pronouns in each of two passages.

  Vague pronouns are explained as those than can refer to more than one antecedent. Example sentences are presented, and a hint box cautions students to avoid repeating the subject as a pronoun. In Practice 4, students correct vague or repeated subject pronoun errors in eight sentences.

  Pronoun shifts are explained as a shift from one point of view to another, including a shift to the second person *you*. A hint box advises students to avoid pronoun shifts in paragraphs. In Practice 5, students correct errors in pronoun shift in eight sentences.

  Pronoun case is defined, and a chart depicting singular and plural forms of subjective, objective, and possessive pronouns is presented. In Practice 6, students identify the pronouns and case of pronouns in eight sentences.

  The section on problems with possessive pronouns covers mistakes with apostrophes for pronouns such as *hers* and *theirs* as well as mistaking contractions for possessive pronouns. A hint box cautions students to think about the possessive, not the object being possessed, in order to use *his* or *her* correctly. In Practice 7, students identify the correct pronouns in three passages.

  Pronoun case rules are presented for pronouns in comparisons with *than* or *as*, pronouns in prepositional phrases, and pronouns with *and* or *or*. A hint box advises students to say the sentence with one pronoun at a time to determine the correct case when there are compound pronouns. In Practice 8, students correct errors in case in ten sentences. In Practice 9, Review, students correct errors in case in three short passages.

  Pronoun case with relative pronouns, including *who* and *whom*, is addressed next. A list of relative pronouns is provided. In a hint box, students are advised to substitute *he/she* or *him/her* for the pronouns *who* and *whom* to help determine the correct pronoun. In Practice 10, students underline the correct relative pronoun in ten sentences. In Practice 11, students identify the correct relative pronoun in three short passages.

  Reflexive pronouns are explained, and examples are provided. In a hint box, students are advised to avoid *hisself* and *theirselves*. In Practice 12, students choose the correct reflexive pronoun for each of nine sentences.

In the Final Review, students edit four paragraphs for pronoun case errors. In The Writer's Room, students are asked to write about one of two topics presented and then identify their pronouns and antecedents. The checklist for pronouns reminds students to use the correct pronoun case in all situations. In The Writer's Circle, students are instructed to work with a partner and write about items in his or her purse or backpack, then exchange paragraphs and check for correct pronoun use. At chapter's end, students are directed to MyWritingLab for further review.

The Writer's World: Sentences and Paragraphs, 3ʳᵈ Edition
CHAPTER 7: PRONOUNS
Exercises

Set 1: Testing Concepts

1. Pronouns are words that
   a. replace nouns, other pronouns, or phrases.
   b. show time, location, or manner.
   c. show action or a state of being.
   d. describe nouns.

2. An *antecedent* is
   a. a word that shows time, location, or manner.
   b. an article that comes before a noun.
   c. a word that the pronoun refers to.
   d. another name for a pronoun.

3. When two or more antecedents are joined by *or* or *nor*, the pronoun must
   a. agree with the nearer antecedent.
   b. agree with the most distant antecedent.
   c. always be plural.
   d. always be singular.

4. A pronoun must agree in person and number with its
   a. adjective.
   b. antecedent.
   c. verb.
   d. preposition.

5. Words such as *each, everybody, everything, nobody, both, others,* and *no one* are called
   a. antecedents.
   b. prepositions.
   c. demonstrative pronouns.
   d. indefinite pronouns.

6. Words such as *each, everybody, everything, nobody,* and *no one* are treated as
   a. singular nouns.
   b. plural nouns.
   c. singular pronouns.
   d. plural pronouns.

7. Words such as *both, few, many, others,* and *several* are treated as
   a. singular nouns.
   b. plural nouns.
   c. singular pronouns.
   d. plural pronouns.

8. A pronoun error that occurs when a pronoun could refer to more than one antecedent is called
   a. a pronoun-antecedent agreement error.
   b. an indefinite pronoun.
   c. a pronoun case error.
   d. a vague pronoun.

9. A pronoun error that occurs when a writer switches from first person to second person is called
   a. a pronoun agreement error.
   b. a pronoun shift.
   c. a pronoun case error.
   d. a vague pronoun.

10. An objective case pronoun functions as the _____ of a sentence or clause.
    a. subject
    b. indefinite pronoun
    c. object
    d. antecedent

11. A subjective case pronoun functions as the _____ of a sentence or clause.
    a. subject
    b. indefinite pronoun
    c. object
    d. antecedent

12. Which of the following pronouns is a possessive pronoun?
    a. we
    b. it's
    c. yours
    d. them

13. If you are unsure about which pronoun case to use in comparisons using *than* or *as,* you can
    a. complete the unwritten thought.
    b. always choose the possessive case.
    c. use whichever pronoun sounds correct to your ear.
    d. always choose the subjective case.

14. When you have more than one pronoun, an easy way to determine the correct case is to
   a. use the objective case because that is the most common pronoun form.
   b. say the sentence with just one pronoun at a time.
   c. use whichever pronoun sounds correct to your ear.
   d. choose the subjective case if the pronoun begins the sentence.

15. Always use the _____ case of a pronoun after a preposition.
   a. objective
   b. possessive
   c. subjective
   d. none of the above

Set 2: Testing Applications

1. Identify the antecedent for the pronoun *their* in the sentence below:

The Johnsons have put their house up for sale.

    a. The Johnsons
    b. have
    c. house
    d. their

2. Identify the antecedent for the pronoun *its* in the sentence below:

At the last minute, the scout troop decided to cancel its car wash fund raiser.

    a. minute
    b. scout
    c. troop
    d. car

3. Choose the correct pronoun for the sentence below:

Juan usually arrives at work several minutes early because _____ likes to have a cup of coffee before beginning his work.

    a. they
    b. it
    c. he or she
    d. he

4. Choose the correct pronoun for the sentence below:

Each of Suki's children has _____ own car.

    a. their
    b. its
    c. his or her
    d. it's

5. Choose the correct pronoun for the sentence below:

The jury is expected to announce _____ verdict today.

    a. their
    b. its
    c. his or her
    d. it's

6. Choose the correct pronoun for the sentence below:

Everybody who attended the workshop had to introduce _____.

    a. himself or herself
    b. themselves
    c. theirselves
    d. theirself

7. Which of the following sentences has a vague pronoun?
    a. Roberto drives his motorcycle to work, no matter what the weather is.
    b. I want to see the movie because it was filmed in my home town.
    c. The committee cancelled its final meeting.
    d. Edward told his father that he needed to buy a new car.

8. Which of the following sentences has a vague pronoun?
    a. Everyone on the team has to pay for his or her own uniforms.
    b. They say that the humidity is worse than the heat.
    c. One of the cats is playing with its tail.
    d. The team will hold its next practice on Saturday.

9. Which sentence uses the pronoun clearly and correctly?
    a. Sheila told her mother that she was invited to a costume party.
    b. Franklin called the radio station, and they told him that he was the tenth caller.
    c. One of the students has left his or her computer bag in the classroom.
    d. After lunch, everyone should bring their plates to the kitchen.

10. Which sentence uses pronouns correctly?
    a. Either Brian or Jeff will give their presentation today.
    b. I was late for work because it was foggy, and you could barely see the road.
    c. Each of my daughters have earned scholarships for college.
    d. One of the employees has parked his or her car in the manager's parking space.

11. Which sentence uses the pronoun correctly?
    a. Juanita said that she would drive Carly and me to the airport.
    b. Him and Keith are going on a motorcycle trip this summer.
    c. You can give the completed report to Jamie or I.
    d. Are you joining Jonathan and I for lunch?

12. Choose the correct pronoun for the blank in the sentence below:
       The directions were quite confusing to Victor and _____.
    a. I
    b. me
    c. myself
    d. we

13. Choose the correct pronoun for the blank in the sentence below:
       Christina is two years younger than _____.
    a. myself
    b. I
    c. him
    d. me

14. Choose the correct pronoun for the blank in the sentence below:

     Customers _____ arrive before noon will receive a discount coupon.

    a. who
    b. whomever
    c. whose
    d. whom

15. Choose the correct pronoun for the blank in the sentence below:

     Between you and _____, his speech was rather boring.

    a. myself
    b. we
    c. I
    d. me

Summary

Chapter 8: Subjects and Verbs covers identifying subjects, prepositional phrases, and verbs. The chapter begins with a grammar snapshot, a short passage with subjects in bold and verbs underlined.

Subjects are divided into singular, plural, compound, pronoun subjects, and gerunds. A hint box explains the difference between simple and complete subjects. In Practice 1, students identify the simple and the complete subject in ten sentences. In Practice 2, students provide a logical subject for the blanks in five sentences.

Special attention is given to unstated (understood) subjects as well as the fact that *here* and *there* are not considered subjects. A hint box advises students to ask themselves who or what the sentence is about to help determine the subject. In Practice 3, students identify simple and unstated subjects in nine sentences.

Prepositional phrases are then introduced; they are explained as words that link nouns, pronouns, and phrases to other words in a sentence. A list of common prepositions is provided. A hint box advises students that the object of a preposition is never the subject of a sentence. In Practice 4, students identify prepositional phrases and subjects in eight sentences. In Practice 5, students identify the subjects in nine sentences.

The final section of this chapter discusses verbs, defined as words that express what the subject does or links the subject to other descriptive words. Action verbs and compound verbs are explained, and examples of each are provided within sentences. In Practice 6, students provide logical verbs in the blanks for six sentences.

Linking verbs are next introduced and are defined as words that describe a state of being or give information about a subject. Examples are provided in sentences, and in Practice 7, students identify the linking verb in eight sentences. A hint box cautions students that infinitive verbs are not main verbs. In Practice 8, students identify subjects and verbs, distinguishing between action verbs and linking verbs.

Helping verbs are explained as those containing two or more verbs and indicate tense, negative structure, or question structure. Examples of *be, have,* and *do* are provided, as well as examples of modals and questions. A hint box advises students that interrupting words and phrases, particularly adverbs, are not part of the verb. In Practice 9, students identify complete verbs in ten sentences.

In the Final Review, students identify subjects and verbs in four passages.

In The Writer's Room, students write about one of two listed subjects and then identify their subjects and verbs. The checklist reminds students how to identify subjects, action verbs, linking verbs, helping verbs, and prepositional phrases. At chapter's end, students are directed to MyWritingLab for further review.

Set 1: Testing Concepts

1. A sentence contains _____ and expresses a complete thought.
    a. both a subject and a verb
    b. either a subject or a verb
    c. a subject
    d. a verb

2. The subject of a sentence
    a. expresses a complete thought.
    b. describes a noun or pronoun.
    c. tells who or what the sentence is about.
    d. expresses an action or state.

3. The verb of a sentence
    a. expresses a complete thought.
    b. describes a noun or pronoun.
    c. tells who or what the sentence is about.
    d. expresses an action or state.

4. A _____ can be the subject of a sentence.
    a. pronoun
    b. gerund
    c. singular noun
    d. all of the above

5. If a sentence is missing either a subject or a verb, it is
    a. considered an incomplete sentence.
    b. considered a command.
    c. considered a complete sentence.
    d. considered a dangling modifier.

6. The simple subject consists of
    a. a thing or the complete name of a person, place, or organization.
    b. the noun plus all the words that describe the verb.
    c. the noun plus all the words that describe the noun.
    d. a thing and the last word of a complete person's name, place, or organization.

7. A complete subject is
   a. the noun plus all the words that describe the verb.
   b. a thing or the complete name of a person, place, or organization.
   c. the noun plus all the words that describe the noun.
   d. a thing and the last word of a complete person's name, place, or organization.

8. In a sentence that expresses a command, such as *Do not park on the grass*, the subject
   a. is the word "grass."
   b. is missing. The sentence is therefore incomplete.
   c. is an "understood" you.
   d. is the word "park."

9. A compound subject consists of
   a. a single noun or pronoun.
   b. a proper name.
   c. a noun or pronoun that is connected by a hyphen.
   d. two or more subjects.

10. In sentences that begin with the words *here* or *there,* the subject
    a. follows the verb.
    b. is unstated.
    c. is *here* or *there*.
    d. is an "understood" you.

11. The verb of a sentence expresses
    a. motion, movement, or position.
    b. an "understood" you.
    c. what the subject does, or it links the subject to other descriptive words.
    d. who or what the subject is.

12. A linking verb describes
    a. mental or physical action.
    b. a state of being.
    c. motion, movement, or position.
    d. who or what the sentence is about.

13. An action verb describes
    a. who or what the sentence is about.
    b. motion, movement, or position.
    c. a state of being.
    d. mental or physical action.

14. A verb beginning with the word "to" is called
    a. an "understood" subject.
    b. a linking verb.
    c. an infinitive verb.
    d. a helping verb.

15. A helping verb
    a. combines with the main verb in order to indicate tense, negative structure, or question structure.
    b. helps to expresses who or what the sentence is about.
    c. begins with the word *to*."
    d. always consists of a single verb.

Set 2: Testing Applications

1. Identify the subject in the following sentence:
   The oak tree is losing its leaves.
      a. oak
      b. tree
      c. its
      d. leaves

2. Identify the subject in the following sentence:
   Mario and his son play golf together quite often.
      a. Mario
      b. son
      c. golf
      d. Mario and his son

3. Identify the subject in the following sentence:
   In the back yard, Bill cooked steaks on the grill.
      a. back yard
      b. Bill
      c. steaks
      d. grill

4. Identify the subject in the following sentence:
   Fishing on Lake Martin is a very pleasant way to spend the morning.
      a. Fishing
      b. Lake Martin
      c. pleasant
      d. morning

5. Identify the complete subject in the sentence below:
   Several rusty old bicycles lay in a heap behind the barn.
      a. Several rusty old bicycles
      b. lay in a heap
      c. bicycles
      d. behind the barn

6. Identify the complete subject in the sentence below:
   The Grand Canyon's new sky walk is an architectural marvel.
      a. The Grand Canyon
      b. new sky walk
      c. The Grand Canyon's new sky walk
      d. an architectural marvel

7. Identify the simple subject in the sentence below:

After a few years, Ted's new sports car will not seem so practical to him.

a. After
b. years
c. sports car
d. car

8. Identify the subject in the sentence below:

Please remember to sign your check.

a. Please
b. remember
c. check
d. "understood you"

9. Identify the simple subject in the sentence below:

Oregon's Crater Lake is the nation's deepest lake.

a. Crater Lake
b. Oregon's
c. lake
d. Oregon's Crater Lake

10. Identify the simple subject in the sentence below:

Here is a book on starting your own business.

a. Here
b. book
c. your
d. business

11. Identify the verb in the sentence below:

George usually drinks two cups of coffee in the morning.

a. George
b. usually
c. drinks
d. coffee

12. Identify the verb in the sentence below:

The main highway to the resort is temporarily closed.

a. highway
b. to
c. temporarily
d. is

13. Identify the verb in the sentence below:

We have been driving for over thirteen hours.
   a. have been driving
   b. have
   c. been driving
   d. have been

14. Identify the main verb in the sentence below:

Oscar decided to order the fried shrimp.
   a. decided
   b. to order
   c. order
   d. decided to

15. Identify the verb in the sentence below:

I wrote Jon a short email and sent it this morning.
   a. wrote
   b. sent
   c. wrote, sent
   d. wrote Jon

The Writer's World: Sentences and Paragraphs, 3rd Edition
CHAPTER 9: PRESENT AND PAST TENSES
Summary

Chapter 9: Present and Past Tenses covers the simple present and past tenses as well as double negatives.

The chapter opens with The Writer's Journal, which asks students to write a short paragraph describing what happened in a spy or suspense movie.

Verb tense is defined as an indication of when an action occurs. Examples are presented, followed by a short discussion of standard vs. nonstandard English in everyday conversation and regions.

The simple present tense is explained, with examples underlined in several sentences. A hint box explains the present progressive tense. Both base forms and third person singular forms are presented. The basic rule for subject-verb agreement is explained, with examples. In Practice 1, students choose the correct verb in ten subject-verb agreement questions.

The simple past tense is introduced, with special mention of regular and irregular verb endings. A hint box explains the past progressive tense. Regular past tense verbs are explained, with examples provided along with a discussion of spelling regular past tense verbs. A hint box explains the difference between *past* and *passed*. In Practice 2, students write the simple past tense form in the blanks for three passages.

Irregular past tense verbs are presented, with examples. In Practice 3, students write the correct forms of regular and irregular verbs in three passages.

The verbs *be* and *have* are explained, with singular and plural examples. In Practice 4, students fill in the correct form of the past tense *be* in two short passages.

Problems with *be*, *have*, and *do*" are discussed, with examples of each. In Practice 5, students correct ten verb errors in three passages.

Negative and question forms are explained, followed by examples and a short note about contractions in academic writing. A hint box explains how to use the correct question and negative forms. In Practice 6, students write questions for five statements. In Practice 7, students create contractions in three passages. A hint box reminds students to use the base form of verbs that follow the infinitive form. In Practice 8, students edit three passages for errors in tense, and spelling.

Double negatives are discussed, and students are shown how to correct them. In Practice 9, students edit two passages for errors in double negatives.

In *Reflect on It*, students are asked to think about what they learned in this chapter and to answer a series of review questions.

In the Final Review, students correct fifteen errors in present tense, past tense, and double negative errors in three paragraphs. In The Writer's Room, students write about one of two topics listed and then check their verb tenses. At chapter's end, students are directed to MyWritingLab for further review.

The Writer's World: Sentences and Paragraphs, 3rd Edition
CHAPTER 9: PRESENT AND PAST TENSES
Exercises

Set 1: Testing Concepts

1. A verb shows
    a. action.
    b. state of being.
    c. position or location.
    d. both a and b2. The common language used and expected in schools, businesses, and government institutions in the United States is called
    a. Standard American English.
    b. Nonstandard English.
    c. Regional English.
    d. jargon.

3. When an action is a general fact or habitual activity, we use the
    a. past tense.
    b. simple present tense.
    c. future tense.
    d. either the past or future tense.

4. Except for the verb *be,* verbs have two forms, which are
    a. standard and nonstandard.
    b. present and future.
    c. base form and third person form.
    d. understood and linking.

5. In the present tense, the subject and verb must
    a. always be a linking verb.
    b. agree in number.
    c. always be an action verb.
    d. be preceded by *to*

6. If the subject is third person singular, such as *he, she,* or *it,* the present tense verb must
    a. have an –*ing* ending.
    b. not have an –*s* ending.
    c. have an –*s* ending.
    d. have an –*ed* ending.

7. Two present tense verbs that are irregular and do not follow the usual pattern for endings are
    a. walk and talk.
    b. drive and sleep.
    c. be and have.
    d. listen and jog.

8. To create present tense questions, begin each question with
    a. have or has.
    b. is or was.
    c. will or who.
    d. do or does.

9. When an action occurred at a specific past time, we use the
    a. simple past tense.
    b. simple present tense.
    c. future tense.
    d. either the simple present tense of the simple past tense.

10. Regular verbs such as *hope* or *cook* have a standard _____ ending to show past tense.
    a. –*ing* ending
    b. –*s* ending
    c. –*ied* or –*ies* ending
    d. –*d* or –*ed* ending

11. All of the following verbs are regular except
    a. look
    b. stay
    c. eat
    d. believe

12. When the subject is plural, and verb is the past tense form of *be*, such as in the following sentence, use
    Daniel and Shane _____ involved in a minor accident.
    a. was
    b. were
    c. be
    d. been

13. When talking about a past event, which form of the word *have*, such as in the following sentence, is correct?

> *Krystal _____ to work a double shift on Saturday.*

    a. had

    b. have

    c. has

    d. having

14. When a writer combines a negative word with a negative adverb, such as in the following incorrect sentence, the error is called

    a. a comma splice.

    b. a dangling modifier.

    c. an irregular verb.

    d. a double negative.

15. The past tense form of the verb *was* is

    a. are.

    b. were.

    c. am.

    d. is.

Set 2: Testing Applications

1. Identify the correct form of the verb for the sentence below:
   The Rose Café now _____ half-price specials before 6:00 p.m.
   a. offered
   b. offer
   c. offers
   d. offering

2. Identify the correct form of the verb for the sentence below:
   Local farmers _____ hoping for rain soon.
   a. are
   b. is
   c. been
   d. be

3. Identify the correct form of the verb for the sentence below:
   Nobody _____ any idea when Marci will be arriving.
   a. have
   b. be having
   c. has
   d. have had

4. Identify the correct form of the verb for the sentence below:
   I believe that it _____ beginning to snow!
   a. were
   b. be
   c. have been
   d. is

5. Identify the correct form of the verb for the sentence below:
   _____ these coupons have an expiration date?
   a. Does
   b. Has
   c. Do
   d. Have

6. Identify the correct form of the verb for the sentence below:
   _____ Chad have your cell phone number?
   a. Do
   b. Does
   c. Is
   d. Has

7. Identify the correct form of the verb for the sentence below:

Amber _____ much television.

    a. don't watch

    b. don't watched

    c. doesn't watch

    d. doesn't watched

8. Identify the correct form of the verb for the sentence below:

_____ your flight leaving on Saturday?

    a. Are

    b. Were

    c. Be

    d. Is

9. Identify the correct form of the verb for the sentence below:

_____ you live on Aspen Avenue?

    a. Don't

    b. Doesn't

    c. Are

    d. Had

10. Identify the correct form of the verb for the sentence below:

How _____ you pronounce your last name?

    a. does

    b. are

    c. do

    d. have

11. Identify the correct form of the verb for the sentence below:

Michelle _____ at a pizza parlor last summer.

    a. worked

    b. work

    c. have work

    d. have worked

12. Identify the correct form of the verb for the sentence below:

Distracted by the radio, I drove _____ my exit.

    a. past

    b. passed

    c. pasted

    d. pass

13. Identify the correct form of the verb for the sentence below:
      Last night, we _____ a stunning sunset.
      a. seen
      b. saw
      c. have saw
      d. had see

14. Identify the correct form of the verb for the sentence below:
      Have you ever _____ on the "Going-to-the-Sun Highway?"
      a. drove
      b. driven
      c. droved
      d. drived

15. Identify the correct form of the verb for the sentence below:
      We must evacuate now. The river _____ to flood.
      a. have begun
      b. has begun
      c. have began
      d. has began

The Writer's World: Sentences and Paragraphs, 3rd Edition
CHAPTER 10: PAST PARTICIPLES
Summary

Chapter 10: Past Participles covers past participles, present perfect tenses, past perfect tenses, past participles as adjectives, and the passive voice. A Grammar Snapshot highlights past participle verbs in a short passage.

Past participles are explained as a verb form, not a verb tense. Examples are provided, and a list of regular verbs and their base, past, and past participle forms is listed. In Practice 1, students identify helping verbs and then fill in the correct form of the verb in ten sentences.

Irregular verbs are then discussed, with a chart that illustrates common forms of irregular verbs in their base, past, and past participle forms. In Practice 2, students fill in the past tense and past participle forms for fifteen verbs. In Practice 3, students edit four passages for errors in past participle verbs.

The present perfect tense is discussed next. Detailed examples of past and present perfect tenses are provided. In Practice 4, students fill in the correct form of present perfect verbs in five short passages. A hint box calls students' attention to time markers that indicate when actions occur. In Practice 5, students choose the correct form of past and present tense verbs in eight sentences. In Practice 6, students fill in the correct form of the simple past or present perfect verbs in three passages.

The past perfect tense is then discussed, with detailed examples provided. In Practice 7, students choose the correct form of the verb in ten sentences. In Practice 8, students identify the correct simple past, present perfect, or past perfect tense in two passages.

The next section explains the use of the past participle as an adjective. An example is provided, and Practice 9 asks students to provide a logical past participle in eight sentences.

The passive voice is introduced, with detailed examples and a chart illustrating how the passive voice differs from the active voice. A hint box cautions students about overusing the passive tense. In Practice 10, students identify verbs as active or passive in two passages. A hint box advises students that in many passive sentences, phrases beginning with *by* are not necessary. In Practice 11, students complete five sentences by changing active verbs to their passive forms. In the same exercise, students change five sentences from the passive voice to the active voice. A hint box advises students that sometimes, the passive form of a verb is suggested but not written. In Practice 12, students edit four passages for errors with past participles.

In the Final Review, students edit fifteen errors with past participles or verb tense in five paragraphs. The Writer's Room asks students to write about one of two topics presented, identify all verbs, and verify that each form is used correctly. A checklist for past participles provides tips to help students ensure that they are using correct verb forms. The chapter ends with a referral to MyWritingLab for supplemental review.

Set 1: Testing Concepts

1. A past participle is a verb form that must be used with
   a. an action verb.
   b. a present tense verb.
   c. a present participle.
   d. a helping verb.

2. The past tense of regular verbs end in
   a. *–s* or *–es.*
   b. *–d* or *–ed.*
   c. *–ing.*
   d. *–ies.*

3. Which sentence contains a past participle?
   a. Mandy has completed her research paper.
   b. We walked five kilometers for the fund raiser.
   c. Are you coming with us to dinner?
   d. Thomas drove from New York to Oregon.

4. Verbs that do not follow the common *–d* or *–ed* endings for the past tense are called
   a. regular verbs.
   b. irregular verbs.
   c. linking verbs.
   d. action verbs.

5. To form the present perfect tense, a past participle is combined with _____
   a. *was* or *were*
   b. *do* or *did*
   c. *is* or *are*
   d. *have* or *has*

6. We use the present perfect tense, such as in the sentence below, to show that an action
   Danielle has been working at the college for five years.
   a. began and ended in the past.
   b. begins in the present and continues.
   c. begins in the present and will end in the near future.
   d. began in the past and continues to the present time.

7. Which sentence contains a present perfect tense?
   a. Are you taking history this semester?
   b. Our family has visited the Grand Canyon several times.
   c. Yesterday, Willard was accepted into the Army.
   d. Have you seen my pet snake?

8. In the sentence below, you can use the present perfect tense to show that
   Since 2005, we have moved three times.
   a. one or more completed actions occurred at unimportant and unspecified times.
   b. an action is occurring at the present time.
   c. an action will continue into the future.
   d. an action has begun but has not yet ended.

9. In the sentence below, you can use the past perfect tense, to show that
   When Jill arrived at the restaurant, we were already eating our dessert.
   a. one or more completed actions occurred at unimportant and unspecified times.
   b. an action has begun and ended in the past.
   c. an action has happened in the past and continues into the future.
   d. a past action happened before another past action.

10. Which sentence contains the past perfect tense?
    a. All of the employees have been trained in the new procedure.
    b. Paul has living in Dallas since 2003.
    c. After they retired, Micah and Denise decided to buy an RV.
    d. When Wayne graduated from high school, he had already earned twelve college credits.

11. A past participle can function as _____, such as in the sentence below.
    Crumpled hamburger wrappers lay on the coffee table.
    a. a verb
    b. an adjective
    c. an adverb
    d. a noun

12. Which sentence contains a past participle that acts as an adjective?
    a. The classroom erupted in a heated discussion about cell phone manners.
    b. In the morning, we were greeted by a brilliant sunset.
    c. The coffee tasted somewhat bitter.
    d. We enjoyed listening to the folk singer at the coffee house.

13. In sentences with the passive voice, such as in the sentence below, the subject
    Derek was advised by his advisor to take trigonometry.
    a. performs the action.
    b. does not perform the action.
    c. is an "understood you."
    d. does not receive the action.

14. To form the passive voice, use the appropriate past tense of the verb _____ + the past participle.
    a. have
    b. do
    c. be
    d. go

15. Which sentence contains the passive voice?
    a. The beach was heavily damaged by the hurricane.
    b. Malcolm stole both third base and home to win the baseball game.
    c. The chocolate chip cookies smelled wonderful to us.
    d. Yesterday afternoon, we picked a basket of apple and made an apple pie.

Set 2: Testing Applications

1. Identify the correct verb for the blank in the sentence below:

     Lyle has _____ the walls of his bedroom a soft beige.
    a. painted
    b. painting
    c. paint
    d. paints

2. Identify the correct verb for the blank in the sentence below:

     I have not _____ Washington, D.C., since I was in high school.
    a. be visiting
    b. visit
    c. visiting
    d. visited

3. Identify the correct verb for the blank in the sentence below:

     Have you already _____ your lunch?
    a. eat
    b. ate
    c. eaten
    d. had eaten

4. Identify the correct verb for the blank in the sentence below:

     Chip's old tractor has _____ down three times this month.
    a. broke
    b. breaked
    c. done broke
    d. broken

5. Identify the correct verb for the blank in the sentence below:

     Victoria claimed that she had _____ across the lake.
    a. swum
    b. swim
    c. swam
    d. swimmed

6. Identify the correct verb for the blank in the sentence below.

     I did not realize that Allison _____ in a plane before now.
    a. had never flew
    b. had never flown
    c. have never flew
    d. have never flying

7. Identify the correct verb for the blank in the sentence below:

We _____ this fishing boat since we were married.

a. have own
b. had own
c. have owned
d. has owned

8. Identify the correct verb for the blank in the sentence below:

Norah _____ her sports car since she graduated from high school.

a. has drove
b. has driven
c. have drove
d. have driven

9. Identify the correct verb for the blank in the sentence below:

Marianna _____ that rash since Tuesday.

a. have had
b. have
c. has have
d. has had

10. Identify the correct verb for the blank in the sentence below:

After we had our car tuned, the engine _____ much better.

a. had performed
b. has performed
c. had perform
d. has perform

11. Identify the correct verb for the blank in the sentence below:

Milton soon realized that the builders _____ substandard materials.

a. had used
b. had use
c. has use
d. has used

12. Identify the correct verb for the blank in the sentence below:

By Monday, the river _____ by two feet.

a. had rose
b. have rose
c. have risen
d. had risen

13. Identify the correct verb for the blank in the sentence below:

    The new furniture _____ yesterday.
    a. was delivered
    b. was deliver
    c. had delivered
    d. been delivered

14. Identify the sentence that uses the active voice.
    a. Jason and Sam reluctantly wore ties to the wedding ceremony.
    b. Belinda's car was purchased in 1990.
    c. These automobile parts are built in Germany.
    d. The film was released in 1980.

15. Identify the sentence that uses the active voice.
    a. My research paper must be turned in by Friday.
    b. The dogs have already been fed.
    c. The children enjoyed their snacks of apples and string cheese.
    d. The restaurant's license was renewed for another year.

The Writer's World: Sentences and Paragraphs, 3rd Edition
CHAPTER 11: PROGRESSIVE TENSES
Summary

Chapter 11: Progressive Tenses addresses present and past progressive tenses, using complete verbs, and other progressive forms. The chapter opens with a Grammar Snapshot, a short passage with progressive verbs underlined.

Progressive tenses are explained, with examples provided. Present progressive tenses are introduced, and examples of those are provided. A chart illustrating affirmative, question, and negative verbs forms are provided. A hint box discusses spelling rules and exceptions for present participles. In Practice 1, students change verbs to the present progressive form in ten sentences.

Simple present and the present progressive tenses are compared, with examples to illustrate. A hint box cautions students about a common tense error: using the progressive tense for action that happens on a regular basis. In Practice 2, students choose the correct verb for each of ten sentences; in addition, they identify the action as a general fact or habit or happening now.

The past progressive tense is introduced, and examples are provided. A chart illustrating the affirmative, question, and negative forms is provided. In Practice 3, students provide the correct past progressive form of the verb in ten sentences.

Using complete verbs is discussed next. Examples are provided, and a hint box cautions students to avoid using the past progressive tense to discuss past habits. In Practice 4, students edit three passages for errors in the progressive tense.

Other progressive forms are introduced: future progressive and present perfect progressive. A hint box lists verbs that do not take the progressive form because they indicate an ongoing state of perception rather than a temporary action. The hint box includes a chart to demonstrate these verbs. Practice 5 asks students to edit ten sentences for errors in verbs.

The final review asks students to correct fifteen errors three passages. In The Writer's Room, students write about one of two topics listed and ensure that they have used verbs correctly. A checklist on progressive verbs gives students tips to check for correct use of progressive verbs. The chapter ends with a recommendation that students go to MyWritingLab for further review.

Set 1: Testing Concepts

1. A verb that was, is, or will be in progress is called
   a. simple past tense verb.
   b. a progressive tense verb.
   c. a future tense verb.
   d. a simple present tense verb.

2. A form of the verb *be* and the present participle *–ing*, as demonstrated in the sentence below, form the
   a. the simple past tense.
   b. the simple present tense.
   c. the past perfect tense.
   d. the progressive tense.

3. The present progressive tense, such as in the following sentence, shows that
       Jody is taking four college courses.
   a. an action is happening now or for a temporary period of time.
   b. an action has begun and ended in the past.
   c. an action will happen in the future.
   d. an action has recently ended.

4. Identify the sentence below that contains the present progressive tense.
   a. Eileen has never been to Australia.
   b. Before moving to Oregon, Deborah had lived in Los Angeles.
   c. Right now, Dave is restoring an antique car.
   d. It rained for three days in a row.

5. In the sentence below, the past progressive tense indicates that
       I was just walking out the apartment door when the phone rang.
   a. an action is occurring now.
   b. an action was in progress at a specific past time or was interrupted.
   c. an began in the past and continues into the future.
   d. an action will occur in the future.

6. Identify the sentence below that contains the past progressive tense.
   a. Kevin was hiking when he broke his ankle.
   b. Our family has owned this shoe store for three generations.
   c. The mayor delivered a rather boring speech.
   d. We are quite concerned about Aunt Martha's health.

7. In progressive forms, always include the complete form of
    a. the action verb.
    b. the base form of the verb.
    c. the helping verb *be*.
    d. the infinitive verb.

8. In progressive forms, make sure that the main verb ends in
    a. *–ed.*
    b. *–s* and *–es.*
    c. *–ies.*
    d. *–ing.*

9. Which sentence below contains a progressive verb?
    a. Stefan offered to repair the sagging steps at his grandparents' house.
    b. Tina and Lori have been friends since the first grade.
    c. Annie nearly missed her flight to Boston.
    d. Burt and Sandra are vacationing in Europe.

10. The future progressive tense, such as in the sentence below, indicates that an action
    I cannot mow the lawn tomorrow because I will be babysitting my niece.
    a. is occurring at the present time.
    b. will be in progress at a future time.
    c. began in the past and will continue into the future.
    d. has already occurred.

11. Identify the sentence below that contains the future progressive tense.
    a. Jewel will be performing in San Diego next month.
    b. It has been snowing since dawn.
    c. William testified at a Congressional hearing.
    d. Our local veterinarian often treats stray dogs and cats.

12. In the sentence below, the present perfect progressive, indicates that an   action
    Monique has been driving for several hours.
    a. is occurring at the present time.
    b. will be in progress at a future time.
    c. has been in progress, without interruption, from a past time up to the present.
    d. began in the past and will continue into the future.

13. Identify the sentence that contains the present perfect progressive.
    a. Elsie was slightly injured in a skiing accident.
    b. The photographer's photos were all out of focus.
    c. Chan has been working at the construction company for several years.
    d. Jessica has finally earned her degree in management.

14. In the sentence below, a nonprogressive verb indicates
    Heather owns a beautiful antique writing desk.
    a. a simple past action.
    b. an ongoing state or a perception.
    c. an action has been in progress, without interruption, from a past time up to the present.
    d. an action that has begun and ended in the past.

15. Identify the sentence below that contains a nonprogressive verb.
    a. Stacy believes in everyday miracles.
    b. Tomorrow we will be planting fruit trees in our yard.
    c. By the time we arrived, the meeting was nearly over.
    d. Last month, Dustin joined the Army.

Set 2: Testing Applications

1. Choose the correct form of the verb for the sentence below:
   Yesterday, we _____ for seven miles over rough terrain.
   a. hike
   b. are hiking
   c. have hiked
   d. hiked

2. Choose the correct form of the verb for the sentence below:
   Our customers typically _____ for sales for major purchases.
   a. wait
   b. waiting
   c. has been waiting
   d. have wait

3. Choose the correct form of the verb for the sentence below:
   We _____ a football game on TV when the power went out.
   a. are watching
   b. watching
   c. were watching
   d. watched

4. Choose the correct form of the verb for the sentence below:
   When Alicia returned to her house, she discovered that a water pipe under the kitchen sink _____.
   a. was leaking
   b. are leaking
   c. were leaking
   d. leaked

5. Choose the correct form of the verb for the sentence below:
   While I _____ dinner, I watched the baseball game on television.
   a. am cooking
   b. was cooking
   c. had cooked
   d. be cooking

6. Choose the correct form of the verb for the sentence below:
   On their recent honeymoon, Jon and Lori _____ at Timberline Lodge in Oregon.
   a. were staying
   b. stay
   c. stayed
   d. had been staying

7. Choose the correct form of the verb for the sentence below:

   Yesterday after class, Professor Moore _____ the campus.
   - a. was leaving
   - b. is leaving
   - c. left
   - d. had left

8. Choose the correct form of the verb for the sentence below:

   Next summer, we _____ our backyard swimming pool.
   - a. will be enjoying
   - b. enjoyed
   - c. enjoy
   - d. had been enjoying

9. Choose the correct form of the verb for the sentence below:

   Ever since Ed retired in June, he _____ early every weekend to watch other workers get on the subway.
   - a. was rising
   - b. have been rising
   - c. rose
   - d. has been rising

10. Choose the correct form of the verb for the sentence below:

    Michael _____ a condo in Destin, Florida.
    - a. is owning
    - b. owns
    - c. has been owning
    - d. own

11. Choose the correct form of the verb for the sentence below:

    Periodically, Dottie and her sister _____ to Europe.
    - a. travel
    - b. travels
    - c. are traveling
    - d. has been traveling

12. Choose the correct form of the verb for the sentence below:

    When Thomas _____ in Colorado, he bought yearly ski passes.
    - a. is living
    - b. has lived
    - c. live
    - d. was living

13. Choose the correct form of the verb for the sentence below:

Abigail _____ her new job, but the commute is over an hour.

a. love
b. has loved
c. loves
d. is loving

14. Choose the correct form of the verb for the sentence below:

Since 1978, the Blackberry Café _____ the best pies in the county.

a. is serving
b. be serving
c. has been serving
d. have been serving

15. Choose the correct form of the verb for the sentence below:

Currently, the personnel office _____ new applications.

a. had not accepted
b. is not accepting
c. have not accepted
d. is not accepted

CHAPTER 12: OTHER VERB FORMS

Summary

Chapter 12: Other Verb Forms discusses modals, the nonstandard forms *gonna, gotta, wanna,* conditional forms, gerunds, and infinitives. The chapter begins with a Grammar Snapshot, a passage with modals in bold print.

Modals are defined as helping verbs that express possibility, advice, and so on. A chart of common modal forms is presented. A hint box advises students that modals have a fixed, consistent form. Practice 1 asks students to indicate the function of underlined modals in ten sentences.

Past and present forms are explained, and special emphasis is given to *can, could will,* and *would.* A hint box discusses the negative forms of modals. In Practice 2, students identify the correct modal forms in five passages.

The past tense of *should, could,* and *would* is discussed, and examples are provided. A hint box cautions students to avoid forms such as *should of* or *shoulda.* Practice 3 asks students to correct eight errors with modal forms in three short passages.

Special attention is given the nonstandard forms of *gonna, gotta,* and *wanna.* Examples of the error and corrections are provided, and a hint box advises students to use the base form of verbs that directly follow modals. In Practice 4, students edit four passages for errors in nonstandard verbs and modal forms.

The next section addresses conditional forms, explained as a sentence containing the word *if* and two clauses. Examples demonstrate conditional forms, and a hint box discusses tense with clauses beginning with the phrase *if I were.* Special note is made of the third conditional form: the impossible past. In Practice 5, students identify the type of conditional sentence for eight sentences. A hint box cautions students to avoid mixing conditional forms. Practice 6 asks students to provide the correct form of verbs in four passages. A hint box addresses common problems with the past conditional, such as using *would have* in the *if* clause. In Practice 7, students edit four passages for errors with conditional forms.

Gerunds and infinitives are introduced, with examples. A chart depicting common verbs and expressions followed by gerunds is presented. Using prepositions and infinitives with gerunds is discussed, and charts are provided for both. In the hint box, special attention is given to *used to.* In Practice 8, students edit eight sentences for errors in gerund and infinitive forms.

For the Final Review, students edit five short passages to correct fifteen errors in verbs. In The Writer's Room, students write about one of two listed topics and ensure that they have formed modals and conditionals correctly. A checklist for other verb forms provides hints to help students form verbs correctly. In The Writer's Circle, a collaborative activity, students work with a group of three to write down all they know about an entertainer. Other students guess the mystery person. The chapter ends with a referral to MyWritingLab for further review.

Set 1: Testing Concepts

1. Modals are _____ that express possibility, advice, and so on.
   a. action verbs
   b. linking verbs
   c. helping verbs
   d. infinitive verbs

2. *Could, might, and may* are all modals that express
   a. a possibility.
   b. an obligation.
   c. advice.
   d. an ability.

3. *Can* is a modal that expresses
   a. an obligation or probability.
   b. a desire.
   c. an ability.
   d. a possibility.

4. *Should* and *ought to* are modals that express
   a. a desire.
   b. an ability.
   c. future action or willingness.
   d. advice.

5. *Must* is a modal that expresses
   a. an ability.
   b. a desire.
   c. an obligation or probability.
   d. advice.

6. All of the following are standard verb forms except
   a. could have.
   b. should of.
   c. should have.
   d. would have.

7. In the sentence below, to form the past tense of *should, could,* and *would,* add *have* and _____

　　　Toby should have checked the oil before he left on his road trip.
   a. the infinitive form of the verb.
   b. the present participle.
   c. the base form of the verb.
   d. the past participle.

8. All of the following are standard verb forms except
   a. going to.
   b. wanna.
   c. want to.
   d. got to.

9. In a conditional sentence, there is
   a. a condition and a result.
   b. a negative structure.
   c. a past participle.
   d. an adverb.

10. In the sentence below, when a condition is true or very possible, use

　　　If you use this coupon, you could save 25%.
   a. the "possible future" form.
   b. the "impossible" present form.
   c. the "impossible past" form.
   d. the "unlikely present" form.

11. In the sentence below, when a condition is not likely and probably will not happen, use

　　　If I won the lottery, I would buy a farm and raise alpacas.
   a. a past participle.
   b. the "possible future" form.
   c. the "unlikely present" form.
   d. the "impossible past" form.

12. In the sentence, below, when the condition cannot happen because the event is over, use

　　　If I had left my house ten minutes earlier, I would not have missed my
flight.
   a. the "possible future" form.
   b. a past participle.
   c. the "unlikely present" form.
   d. the "impossible past" form.

13. A *gerund* is a verb
    a. that consists of *to–* and the base form of the verb.
    b. that indicates the past tense.
    c. with an *–ing* ending.
    d. all of the above

14. An *infinitive* is a verb
    a. that consists of *to–* and the base form of the verb.
    b. with an *–ing* ending.
    c. that indicates the past tense.
    d. all of the above.

15. In the sentence below, if the verb has a *verb + preposition + object,* the second verb is _____.
    > *Carl is thinking about buying a boat.*
    a. an infinitive
    b. a gerund
    c. a past tense verb
    d. a present tense verb

Set 2: Testing Applications

1. Choose the correct verb form for the blank in the sentence below:
    Following my graduation this coming spring, I _____ move to Colorado.
    a. would
    b. have
    c. did
    d. can

2. Choose the correct verb form for the blank in the sentence below:
    Some day, Maxwell _____ like to visit New Zealand.
    a. would
    b. can
    c. could
    d. will

3. Choose the correct verb form for the blank in the sentence below:
    My home made pizza was good, but I _____ used more cheese.
    a. would have
    b. should of
    c. should have
    d. could of

4. Choose the correct verb form for the blank in the sentence below:
    If we had known you wanted a kitten, we _____ you one from the farm.
    a. had given
    b. would have given
    c. would give
    d. would of given

5. Choose the correct verb form for the blank in the sentence below:
    You _____ seen Deborah's face when she opened her gift.
    a. shoulda
    b. should have
    c. would of
    d. should had

6. Choose the correct verb form for the blank in the sentence below:
    If you wish, you _____ my fishing pole on Saturday.
    a. borrow
    b. could borrowed
    c. should have borrowed
    d. may borrow

7. Choose the correct verb form for the blank in the sentence below:

If Damian does well at the singing audition next Saturday, he _____ to Hollywood.

    a. will have gone
    b. be going
    c. going
    d. will be going

8. Choose the correct verb form for the blank in the sentence below:

If Joseph had not washed his white clothes with the red towels, he _____ his t-shirts pink.

    a. would not have turned
    b. would turn
    c. could turn
    d. will not have turn

9. Choose the correct verb form for the blank in the sentence below:

If we had our own skiing equipment, we _____ to rent it.

    a. would not have
    b. would not of
    c. could not had
    d. could not have

10. Choose the correct verb form for the blank in the sentence below:

If Rosie were not afraid of flying, she _____ her cousin in Hawaii.

    a. would visited
    b. will visit
    c. could have visit
    d. would visit

11. Choose the correct verb form for the blank in the sentence below:

If I _____ Brett, I would not invest in Steve's proposed company.

    a. am
    b. was
    c. were
    d. be

12. Choose the correct verb form for the blank in the sentence below:

If Andrew had remembered to set his alarm, he _____.

    a. would not have overslept.
    b. would have overslept.
    c. would not of overslept.
    d. could not had overslept.

13. Choose the correct verb form for the blank in the sentence below:

    If that cell phone _____ less expensive, I would buy it.
    a. were
    b. had been
    c. is
    d. would have been

14. Choose the correct verb form for the blank in the sentence below:

    My sister has decided _____ to New York City.
    a. to have moved
    b. to moved
    c. to be moving
    d. to move

15. Choose the correct verb form for the blank in the sentence below:

    Mom _____ tennis lessons every Wednesday at the YMCA.
    a. is take
    b. be taking
    c. is taking
    d. had took

Summary

Chapter 13: Subject-verb Agreement, covers basic subject-verb agreement rules and the following: verbs before subjects, more than one subject, special subject forms, and interrupting words and phrases. The chapter opens with a Grammar Snapshot, a passage in which the subjects are in bold print and the verbs are underlined.

Basic subject-verb agreement rules are covered first: subject-verb agreement with simple present tense. Examples are provided, and a chart illustrates the singular and plural forms with first, second, and third person. In Practice 1, students choose the correct verb in ten sentences.

Special note is made of troublesome present tense verbs: *be, have,* and *do*. A chart illustrates the correct forms, and in Practice 2, students provide the correct verb in two passages. In Practice 3, students edit two passages for subject-verb agreement errors.

Agreement in other tenses is discussed next. Examples are provided for agreement with simple past tense and the present tense form of *be*. The present perfect tense and other tenses are also covered. In Practice 4, students identify the correct verb in ten sentences.

Verbs before subjects are covered next: sentences beginning with *there* and *here* as well as questions. Examples are provided, and Practice 5 asks students to identify both the subject and the correct verb in ten sentences. In Practice 6, students identify subject-verb agreement errors in eight sentences.

The next section discusses more than one subject, and examples are provided. In Practice 7, students identify the subject and the correct verb in ten sentences.

Special subject forms are introduced. The first is indefinite pronouns. A chart of singular and plural pronouns is presented, with examples of each. Practice 8 asks students to identify both the subject and the correct verb in four passages. Special subject forms also include collective nouns as subjects. A list of common collective nouns is provided, and Practice 9 asks students to identify the subject and the correct verb in three passages.

The final section covers interrupting words and phrases. Examples of interrupting prepositional phrases are provided, and a hint box advises students to place parentheses around interrupting words and phrases to help identify the subject. In Practice 10, students place parentheses around interrupting words and phrases and then choose the correct form of the verb. In Practice 11, students edit ten sentences for subject-verb agreement errors. Special note is made of the interrupting words *who, which,* and *that.* Examples are provided, and Practice 12 asks students to identify the correct verb forms in two passages.

The Final Review asks students to edit three passages for errors in subject-verb agreement. In The Writer's Room, students write about one of two listed topics, identify each subject, and ensure that all subjects and verbs agree. The subject-verb agreement checklist reminds students of the subject-verb agreement rules. At chapter's end, students are referred to MyWritingLab for further review.

Set 1: Testing Concepts

1. Subject-verb agreement means that
     a. a singular subject needs a singular verb.
     b. a plural subject needs a plural verb.
     c. a subject and verb must agree in number.
     d. all of the above.

2. Use the simple present tense when an action
     a. will occur in the future.
     b. has occurred in the past.
     c. is habitual or factual.
     d. began and ended in the past.

3. In the third-person singular form, the subject can be
     a. *they, them,* or *us.*
     b. *he, she,* or *it.*
     c. *his, hers, theirs,* or *ours.*
     d. any of the above.

4. When the subject is the third-person singular form,
     a. add *–s* or *–es* to the verb.
     b. add *–d* or *–ed* to the verb.
     c. add a past participle after the verb.
     d. do not add an ending to the verb.

5. When the subject is *I, you, we, they,* or the equivalent (*the Smiths, the books, Jay and I*),
     a. add *–d* or *–ed* to the verb.
     b. add a past participle after the verb.
     c. add *–s* or *–es* to the verb.
     d. do not add an ending to the verb.

6. In the simple past tense, all verbs except _____ have one past form.
     a. ride
     b. wonder
     c. visit
     d. be

7. In the present perfect tense, such as in the sentence below, use _____ if the subject is third-person singular.

> *He has never learned how to drive a standard transmission.*

    a. have
    b. has
    c. have been
    d. were

8. When the verb comes before the subject, the subject and the verb must
    a. must always be singular.
    b. must always be plural.
    c. agree.
    d. not agree.

9. When a sentence begins with *there* or *here*, the subject
    a. is *there* or *here*.
    b. agrees with *there* or *here*.
    c. comes before the verb.
    d. follows the verb.

10. Generally, when two subject are joined by *and,* use
    a. the plural form of the verb.
    b. the singular form of the verb.
    c. the infinitive form of the verb.
    d. either the singular or the plural form of the verb.

11. When two or more subjects are joined by *or* or *nor,* the verb
    a. always takes the plural form.
    b. agrees with the first subject.
    c. agrees with the closer subject.
    d. always takes the singular form.

12. Indefinite pronouns, such as *anybody, each, everyone,* and *something* are treated as
    a. plural.
    b. singular.
    c. either singular or plural.
    d. neutral.

13. Indefinite pronouns such as *both, few, several,* and *many* are treated as
    a. plural.
    b. singular.
    c. either singular or plural.
    d. neutral.

14. Collective nouns, which are generally treated as singular, are words like
   a. *each, nobody,* and *everyone.*
   b. *Miami, Wahtonka High School,* and *the Columbia River.*
   c. *you, it,* and *I.*
   d. *family, band,* and *class.*

15. If a sentence contains a clause beginning with *who, which,* or *that,* such as in the sentence below, the verb
   We recently met a man who plays professional football.
   a. agrees with the word preceding *who, which,* or *that.*
   b. agrees with the subject preceding *who, which,* or *that.*
   c. is always singular.
   d. is always plural.

Set 2: Testing Applications

1. In which sentence is the verb used incorrectly?
        a. The oak table and chairs are all on sale.
        b. In good weather, Matthew rides his bicycle to work.
        c. All of our employees plans to attend the banquet.
        d. Usually, the scout troop meets at our house.

2. In which sentence is the verb used incorrectly?
        a. I believe they are friends of Benjamin.
        b. Calvin and I was classmates in college.
        c. I am quite content with my job.
        d. You are from California, aren't you?

3. Choose the correct verb for the blanks in the following sentence:
        Lisa and her family _____ that their art collection _____ worth a lot of money.
        a. think, is
        b. thinks, are
        c. think, are
        d. thinks, is

4. Choose the correct verb for the blanks in the following sentence:
        Because my favorite sandwich shop _____ gone out of business, I _____ started bringing my own lunch to work.
        a. has, has
        b. have, have
        c. have, has
        d. has, have

5. Choose the correct verb for the blanks in the following sentence:
        Annie's two sons _____ considering moving back home because they _____ lost their jobs.
        a. are, has
        b. are, have
        c. is, have
        d. is, has

6. Choose the correct verb for the blanks in the following sentence:
        Someone in our office _____ discovered that some funds _____ being misused.
        a. have, are
        b. has, is
        c. has, are
        d. have, is

7. Choose the correct verb for the blanks in the following sentence:

Each of the contestants _____ to hear if his or her answer _____ correct.

    a. waits, are
    b. wait, is
    c. waits, is
    d. wait, are

8. Choose the correct verb for the blanks in the following sentence:

_____ the workers remembered that there _____ expense reports due tomorrow?

    a. Have, is
    b. Have, are
    c. Has, is
    d. Has, are

9. Choose the correct verb for the blanks in the following sentence:

_____ the detectives really suspect that our neighbor _____ banks?

    a. Do, robs
    b. Do, rob
    c. Does, robs
    d. Does, rob

10. Choose the correct verb for the blanks in the following sentence:

_____ this pink blouse _____ with this skirt?

    a. Do, go
    b. Do, goes
    c. Does, go
    d. Does, goes

11. Choose the correct verb for the blanks in the following sentence:

Either Jake or Luther _____ the lawn, but everybody _____ turns washing the dishes.

    a. mows, take
    b. mow, takes
    c. mow, take
    d. mows, takes

12. Choose the correct verb for the blanks in the following sentence:

The condition of the carpets in our house _____ poor, but the estimates for replacement _____ very high.

    a. are, seem
    b. are, seems
    c. is, seem
    d. is, seems

13. Choose the correct verb for the blanks in the following sentence:

Professor Smyth, along with her students, _____ meeting in a
computer lab where each of them _____ an individual computer.
       a. prefer, have
       b. prefer, has
       c. prefers, have
       d. prefers, has

14. Choose the correct verb for the blanks in the following sentence:

Each of the entrees on the menu _____ with dessert, but neither of
us ever _____ it.
       a. come, orders
       b. come, order
       c. comes, orders
       d. comes, order

15. Choose the correct verb for the blanks in the following sentence:

There _____ three movies that I want to see at the theater, and one
of them _____ my favorite actor.
       a. are, star
       b. are, stars
       c. is, star
       d. are, stars

The Writer's World: Sentences and Paragraphs, 3rd Edition
CHAPTER 14: TENSE CONSISTENCY
Summary

Chapter 14: Tense Consistency covers consistent verb tense. The chapter opens with a Grammar Snapshot of a passage with verbs underlined.

Verb tense shifts are explained as those that are illogical and confusing to the reader. An example of an illogical tense shift, followed by the correction, is provided. In Practice 1, students identify the verb in each of twelve sentences and then determine whether the verb maintains consistent tense. A hint box advises students to use *would* and *could* when telling a story about a past event. In Practice 2, students correct six tense inconsistencies in two paragraphs.

Using past and present tense when telling a story is discussed, and examples are shown of each. Practice 3 asks students to edit a paragraph for consistent tense.

The Final Review asks students to edit four paragraphs for fifteen tense inconsistencies. In The Writer's Room, students write about one of two listed topics and ensure that their verb tenses are consistent. The tense consistency checklist provides hints to help students check for tense shifts. In The Writer's Circle, students survey people about several questions, then write about the results, ensuring that their verb tenses are consistent. At chapter's end, students are directed to MyWritingLab for further review.

Set 1: Testing Concepts

1. Verb tense indicates
    a. how an event occurred.
    b. whether the verb expresses mental or physical action.
    c. whether the verb expresses action or a state of being.
    d. when an event occurred.

2. A tense shift error occurs when you
    a. shift from one tense to another for no logical reason.
    b. shift from an action to a linking verb.
    c. shift from a regular verb to an irregular verb.
    d. all of the above

3. When you tell a story about a past event, use _____ instead of *will* and *can*.
    a. *will be* and *could*
    b. *would* and *could*
    c. *had* and *could be*
    d. *would* and *could be*

4. When you tell a story, you can describe events using the _____ tense.
    a. past
    b. present
    c. future
    d. all of the above

5. The present tense is used when the action
    a. is about to occur.
    b. is habitual or factual.
    c. has not yet occurred.
    d. has begun and ended in the past.

6. The past tense is used when the action
    a. has occurred in the past.
    b. is habitual or factual.
    c. is about to occur.
    d. has begun and continues into the future.

7. The future tense is used when the action
    a. is habitual or factual.
    b. is currently happening.
    c. has occurred in the past.
    d. will happen at some point in the future.

8. When you tell a story, your verb tenses must be _____ .
    a. varied
    b. in the past tense
    c. consistent
    d. in the present tense

9. Identify the tense of the verb in the sentence below:
    For breakfast, Maria usually has a fruit smoothie.
    a. present
    b. past
    c. future
    d. progressive

10. Identify the tense of the verb in the sentence below:
    In 2005, we adopted two Siamese kittens.
    a. present
    b. past
    c. future
    d. progressive

11. Identify the tense of the verb in the sentence below:
    Our train will be leaving at 3:45 p.m.
    a. present
    b. past
    c. future
    d. progressive

12. Identify the present tense form of the verb *to call.*
    a. call
    b. called
    c. will call
    d. should have called

13. Identify the past tense form of the verb *to write.*
    a. is writing
    b. will be writing
    c. write
    d. wrote

14. Identify the future tense form of the verb *to go*.
    a. went
    b. has gone
    c. will go
    d. has been going

15. Identify the past tense form of the verb *to think*.
    a. will think
    b. thought
    c. is thinking
    d. will be thinking

Set 2: Testing Applications

1. Choose the correct verb for the blank in the sentence below:
        Jon and Lori are getting married in the spring, and they _____ to spend their honeymoon in Greece.
        a. planned
        b. are planning
        c. is planning
        d. have plan

2. Choose the correct verb for the blank in the sentence below:
        Last year, Ted _____ his leg in a skiing accident.
        a. broke
        b. breaks
        c. had broke
        d. break

3. Choose the correct verb for the blank in the sentence below:
        Tonya used to live in Maine, but now she _____ in Florida.
        a. has lived
        b. be living
        c. lived
        d. is living

4. Choose the correct verb for the blank in the sentence below:
        I find it strange that both my sisters _____ chocolate.
        a. are disliking
        b. dislike
        c. have dislike
        d. be disliking

5. Choose the correct verb for the blank in the sentence below:
        If we had not stayed up so late last night, we _____ not be so tired today.
        a. can
        b. will
        c. would
        d. might will

6. Choose the correct verb for the blank in the sentence below:
        Windsurfers flock to the Columbia River Gorge because the wind _____ consistently strong.
        a. is
        b. be
        c. has been
        d. are being

111

7. Choose the correct verb for the blank in the sentence below:

The flood damaged the bridge, so we _____ a detour this morning.

a. had to take
b. have took
c. will have taken
d. should have took

8. Choose the correct verb for the blank in the sentence below:

If Jamal had attended the orientation for the online literature course, he _____ about the procedure for submitting homework.

a. had learned
b. would be learning
c. would have learned
d. had been learning

9. Choose the correct verb for the blank in the sentence below:

Amanda used to take the freeway to work, but now she _____ a longer but more scenic route around the lake.

a. has taken
b. took
c. had been taking
d. takes

10. Choose the correct verb for the blank in the sentence below:

Although Victor reviewed his notes, he _____ the algebra problem until he met with his professor.

a. has not understood
b. did not understand
c. is not understanding
d. does not understand

11. Choose the correct verb for the blank in the sentence below:

If you had known that Dennis was in a bad mood, would you _____ him?

a. had teased
b. be teasing
c. have teased
d. tease

12. Choose the correct verb for the blank in the sentence below:

When Ellen was a child, she _____ Elvis Presley one day in a café.

a. met
b. meet
c. is meeting
d. will have met

13. Choose the correct verb for the blank in the sentence below:
    If I were you, I _____ to college.
    a. would returned
    b. will return
    c. will be returning
    d. would return

14. Choose the correct verb for the blank in the sentence below:
    Whenever my cat sees a squirrel, she _____.
    a. growled
    b. was growling
    c. would growl
    d. growls

15. Choose the correct verb for the blank in the sentence below:
    We were frightened when we _____ that the hurricane was headed our way.
    a. learn
    b. learned
    c. have learned
    d. are learning

The Writer's World: Sentences and Paragraphs, 3rd Edition
CHAPTER 15: COMPOUND SENTENCES

Summary

Chapter 15: Compound Sentences addresses the use of compound sentences to vary sentence structure. This chapter discusses simple versus compound sentences, and combining sentences using coordinating conjunctions, semicolons, and transitional expressions. The chapter opens with a Grammar Snapshot, a paragraph in which compound sentences are underlined.

Simple sentences are compared with compound sentences as a way of varying sentence structure, and examples are provided for illustration.

Combining sentences using coordinating conjunctions is introduced, with an example illustrating the seven coordinating conjunctions. A hint box advises students to place a finger over the coordinator to help determine whether the two clauses are complete sentences. In Practice 1, students identify eight sentences as either simple or compound sentences.

Definitions for each coordinating conjunction are explained, with a chart showing function and an example. In Practice 2, students add a comma and an appropriate coordinating conjunction to join eight pairs of sentences. In Practice 3, students create compound sentences by adding a coordinating conjunction and another complete sentence to each of five sentences. In Practice 4, students join eight pairs of sentences using coordinating conjunctions in two paragraphs.

Combining sentences using semicolons is introduced next. An example of a compound sentence joined by a semicolon is presented. In Practice 5, students place a semicolon in the appropriate place in eight sentences. A hint box advises students to use the semicolon to join related ideas. In Practice 6, students create compound sentences by adding a semicolon and another complete sentence to five simple sentences.

Combining sentences using transitional expressions is presented. A chart illustrates common transitional expressions and their meanings. Punctuation for transitional expressions is explained, and in Practice 7, students add necessary semicolons and commas to transitions in seven sentences. In Practice 8, students create five compound sentences by choosing appropriate transitional expressions for each. Practice 9 asks students to create six compound sentences by adding logical transitional expressions.

In the Final Review, students revise four passages by creating compound sentences. In The Writer's Room, students write about one of two topics listed, then combine some of their sentences to create compound sentences. A checklist provides punctuation hints for compound sentences. The chapter ends with a referral to MyWritingLab for further review.

Set 1: Testing Concepts

1. One way to make your writing more appealing is to
    a. repeat descriptive words.
    b. use all short sentences.
    c. use sentences of varying length.
    d. use all long sentences.

2. One of the easiest ways to create sentence variety is to
    a. combine simple sentences to form compound sentences.
    b. change compound sentences to simple sentences.
    c. make your sentences about the same length.
    d. change complex sentences to simple sentences.

3. A compound sentence contains
    a. an incomplete idea.
    b. one simple sentence.
    c. at least three complete ideas.
    d. two or more simple sentences.

4. Two simple sentences can be joined in all of the following ways except
    a. a semicolon.
    b. a comma.
    c. a period.
    d. a comma and coordinating conjunction.

5. When you combine two sentences with a comma,
    a. you must also use a coordinating conjunction after the comma.
    b. you must also use a coordinating conjunction before the comma.
    c. you must not use a coordinating conjunction.
    d. you must not use any other conjunctions.

6. The coordinating conjunction *for* is used to
    a. join two ideas.
    b. indicate a reason.
    c. offer an alternative.
    d. contrast two ideas.

7. The coordinating conjunction *but* is used to
     a. indicate a cause-effect relationship.
     b. indicate a reason.
     c. offer an alternative.
     d. contrast two ideas.
8. The coordinating conjunction *or* is used to
     a. join two ideas.
     b. indicate a cause-effect relationship.
     c. offer an alternative.
     d. introduce a surprising idea.

9. The coordinating conjunction *yet* is used to
     a. indicate a negative idea.
     b. offer an alternative.
     c. indicate a cause-effect relationship.
     d. introduce a surprising idea.

10. The coordinating conjunction *nor* is used to
     a. indicate a negative idea.
     b. offer an alternative.
     c. indicate a cause-effect relationship.
     d. introduce a surprising idea.

11. A semicolon can replace
     a. a comma.
     b. a dash.
     c. a subordinating conjunction.
     d. a conjunction.

12. A transitional expression that shows contrast is
     a. however.
     b. also.
     c. eventually.
     d. therefore.

13. A transitional expression that shows a result or consequence is
     a. on the other hand.
     b. consequently.
     c. furthermore.
     d. finally.

14. A transitional expression that shows an alternative is
     a. moreover.
     b. on the other hand.
     c. furthermore.
     d. however.

15. If the second sentence begins with a transitional expression,
    a. put a comma before the transition.
    b. put a comma before the transition and a semicolon after it.
    c. put a semicolon after the transition.
    d. put a semicolon before the transition and a comma after it.

Set 2: Testing Applications

1. Which of the following sentences is a simple sentence?
       a. Julie sells beautiful stained glass decorations at craft fairs.
       b. It's cloudy outside, but the temperature is very pleasant.
       c. I need new shoes, so I am going to the mall today.
       d. The postal carrier is at the door, and he has a package for you.

2. Which of the following sentences is a compound sentence?
       a. On the top shelf in the living room closet, you will find my old typewriter.
       b. Have you ever been to Australia?
       c. Our hiking club has decided to hike the John Muir Trail next summer.
       d. The chicken strips come with French fries, but you may substitute a salad.

3. Which coordinating conjunction is the most appropriate for the sentence below?
       Les bought Maria a box of chocolates, _____ he has a crush on her.
     a. so
     b. for
     c. or
     d. but

4. Which coordinating conjunction is the most appropriate for the sentence below?
       The vase had a small chip, _____ the manager gave me a discount.
     a. or
     b. but
     c. so
     d. for

5. Which compound sentence is punctuated correctly?
       a. I remember the ugly duckling, it became a swan.
       b. You are welcome to have some coffee but, we are out of cream.
       c. Everyone seems to be happy we can feel the first hint of fall in the air.
       d. Katy visited New York on vacation, and now she wants to move there.

6. Which compound sentence is punctuated correctly?
       a. I'm very tired; I have been cleaning house all day.
       b. The burritos at Mi Casa Café are excellent; and the prices are reasonable, too.
       c. Fall weather will be here soon leaves are already falling from the oak trees.
       d. The surf is up so we are all headed for the beach.

7. Which compound sentence is punctuated correctly?
a. Our trip to the Australian animal reserve was the highlight of our trip we got to hold a koala bear.
       b. We discovered a large snake in the garden, but it was not a poisonous one.
       c. Latonya is my best friend she believes in all my crazy dreams.
       d. Maya does not eat beef nor does she eat chicken or fish.

8. Which compound sentence is punctuated correctly?
a. You should buy your computer from a large electronics retailer the prices are much better.
   b. I do not have time to go skiing this winter; nor can I afford it.
   c. The matinee doesn't start at noon; it starts at 1:00 p.m.
   d. We hid our dog's medicine in a piece of steak yet he still spit out the pill.

9. Which transitional expression is the best choice for the following sentence?
   Blake forgot to study for his psychology exam; _____, *he received a low grade.*
   a. on the other hand
   b. therefore
   c. nevertheless
   d. however

10. Which transitional expression is the best choice for the following sentence?
    Beverly loves her new job; _____, *the salary is quite low.*
    a. however
    b. therefore
    c. consequently
    d. on the contrary

11. Which transitional expression is the best choice for the following sentence?
    The truck camper is less expensive and is more maneuverable;
    _____, *the travel trailer has much more room.*
    a. furthermore
    b. consequently
    c. moreover
    d. on the other hand

12. Which transitional expression is the best choice for the following sentence?
    Our instructor has been teaching digital photography for ten years;
    _____, *her work has won many prestigious awards.*
    a. furthermore
    b. finally
    c. on the contrary
    d. for instance

13. Which compound sentence is punctuated correctly?
a. The weather forecaster has predicted light rain for Saturday nevertheless, we will hold our garage sale.
b. Jennifer chopped vegetables for the salad meanwhile, the chicken was baking in the oven.
c. Shane found a great airline fare online; however, he had four connections with long layovers.
d. There is thick fog outside, therefore, you will need to leave for work early.

14. Which compound sentence is punctuated correctly?
    a. Sugarland is coming to our city and we have front row tickets.
    b. We are sorry for our error; however, we cannot refund your money.
    c. Dan is an adventurer, in fact, he hiked the Appalachian Trail last year.
    d. Dogs are not allowed on this beach so, we must leave Spunky at home.

15. Which compound sentence is punctuated correctly?
    a. I can't hear what you are saying, a jet is flying overhead.
    b. You may prepay your order, or you may pay when it arrives.
    c. Allan paid for our admission to the zoo furthermore, he bought us all lunch.
    d. The quarterly report is not finished; therefore, we all must work late this week.

The Writer's World: Sentences and Paragraphs, 3rd Edition
CHAPTER 16: COMPLEX SENTENCES
Summary

Chapter 16: Complex Sentences covers understanding complex sentences, using subordinating conjunctions, using relative pronouns, and combining questions. The chapter opens with a Grammar Snapshot, a paragraph with complex sentences underlined.

Complex sentences are explained as a sentence containing one independent clause and one or more dependent clauses. Examples are provided, and a hint box introduces compound-complex sentences.

The use of subordinating conjunctions is explained, and a list of common subordinating conjunctions is provided. A chart illustrates the use of some of the most common subordinating conjunctions, and examples of those are provided. In Practice 1, students identify the dependent clause and the subordinating conjunctions for each of six sentences. A hint box advises students to avoid using a comma before a subordinating conjunction in the middle of a sentence. Practice 2 asks students to identify subordinating conjunctions in a passage. In Practice 3, students supply missing subordinating conjunctions in three passages. A hint box reminds students to put a subject after the subordinator when combining sentences to form complex sentences. In Practice 4, students add missing subjects in two passages. In Practice 5, students practice combining two independent clauses by using one of the listed subordinators for each of four pairs of sentences.

Using relative pronouns to form complex sentences is addressed next. Examples are provided, and a hint box explains how to punctuate relative clauses. In Practice 6, students identify the relative pronoun in a passage. In Practice 7, students combine five sets of sentences using relative pronouns. In Practice 8, students add dependent clauses beginning with relative pronouns to each of five sentences.

Combining sentences by creating embedded questions is introduced, and examples are provided. A hint box advises students to ensure that they have used the correct word order for imbedded questions. In Practice 9, students create new sentences for each of five questions. In Practice 10, students identify and correct errors with embedded questions in three passages.

In the Final Review, students revise two paragraphs for sentence variety by forming complex sentences. In The Writer's Room, students write about one of two listed topics, ensuring that they have formed and punctuated their complex sentences correctly. The complex sentences checklist provides hints for students to check their sentences for correct structure and punctuation. The chapter ends with a referral to MyWritingLab for further review.

The Writer's World: Sentences and Paragraphs, 3rd Edition
CHAPTER 16: COMPLEX SENTENCES
Exercises

Set 1: Testing Concepts

1. A sentence containing one independent clause and one or more dependent clauses is known as
        a. a simple sentence.
        b. a compound sentence.
        c. a complex sentence.
        d. a compound-complex sentence.

2. An independent clause expresses a complete idea and contains
        a. a subject but not necessarily a verb.
        b. a subject and a verb.
        c. a verb but not necessarily a subject.
        d. either a subject or a verb but not both.

3. A word group that expresses an incomplete idea is called
        a. a dependent clause.
        b. an independent clause.
        c. a complex sentence.
        d. a compound sentence.

4. A sentence that contains two or more independent clauses and one or more dependent clauses is called
        a. a simple sentence.
        b. a compound sentence.
        c. a complex sentence.
        d. a compound-complex sentence.

5. You can turn an independent clause into a dependent clause by adding
        a. an adverb, such as *later, tomorrow,* or *finally.*
        b. a subordinating conjunction such as *because, after,* or *although.*
        c. a coordinating conjunction such as *and, but,* or *so.*
        d. a conjunctive adverb such as *however, therefore,* or *moreover.*

6. Subordinating conjunctions are words that introduce
        a. secondary ideas.
        b. primary ideas.
        c. transitions.
        d. all of the above.

7. Which of the following words is NOT a subordinating conjunction?
   a. since
   b. because
   c. therefore
   d. although

8. If you use a subordinating conjunction at the beginning of a sentence,
   a. do not use a comma.
   b. put a comma after the subordinating conjunction.
   c. put a comma after the subordinating conjunction and after the dependent sentence.
   d. put a comma after the dependent sentence.

9. Generally, if you use a subordinating conjunction in the middle of the sentence, such as in the sentence below,
   I went to Brad's party although I did not really want to go.
   a. do not use a comma.
   b. put a comma after the dependent sentence.
   c. put a comma after the subordinating conjunction.
   d. put a comma after the subordinating conjunction and after the dependent sentence.

10. A relative pronoun
    a. is a conjunctive adverb.
    b. describes a noun or pronoun.
    c. is a coordinating conjunction.
    d. describes a verb or adjective.

11. Which of the following is NOT a relative pronoun?
    a. who
    b. that
    c. which
    d. because

12. If a relative clause contains nonessential information,
    a. commas are optional.
    b. use commas to set it off.
    c. do not use commas to set it off.
    d. use a comma after the relative pronoun.

13. If a relative clause contains essential information,
    a. do not use commas to set it off.
    b. use commas to set it off.
    c. use a comma after the relative pronoun.
    d. commas are optional.

14. Which of the following sentences includes an embedded question?
    a. Nobody understood why Blake decided to quit his job.
    b. Will you be joining us for dinner?
    c. Have you finished raking the yard yet?
    d. We will have to question the regional manager about the policy changes.

15. Which of the following sentences is structured incorrectly?
    a. I have no idea why the mail was not picked up today.
    b. Very few customers understand how to apply for the rebate.
    c. Theodore asked me why did I miss class last week?
    d. Have you ever seen how a hay baler works?

Set 2: Testing Applications

1. Identify the underlined portion of the sentence below:

        We had to dilute our coffee with water <u>because it was so strong</u>.
    a. coordinating conjunction
    b. subordinating conjunction
    c. independent clause
    d. dependent clause

2. Identify the underlined portion of the sentence below:

        After we reached the summit of the mountain, <u>we could see the entire valley below us.</u>
    a. coordinating conjunction
    b. subordinating conjunction
    c. independent clause
    d. dependent clause

3. Identify the underlined portion of the sentence below:

        Byron's comment was funny <u>even though</u> it was a bit unkind.
    a. coordinating conjunction
    b. subordinating conjunction
    c. independent clause
    d. dependent clause

4. Choose the most effective subordinating conjunction for the blank in the sentence below:

        _____ *my brother is cooking dinner tonight, I volunteered to do the dishes.*
    a. Since
    b. Until
    c. Even though
    d. Although

5. Choose the most effective subordinating conjunction for the blank in the sentence below:

        _____ *Damian does not arrive in fifteen minutes, we will leave for the beach without him.*
    a. Unless
    b. Because
    c. If
    d. Even though

6. Choose the most effective subordinating conjunction for the blank in the sentence below:

_____ *the author's speech lasted over an hour, the audience remained attentive.*

 a. If
 b. After
 c. Even though
 d. Unless

7. Which sentence is punctuated correctly?
 a. The rose bush seems to be thriving although, it is often neglected.
 b. The rose bush seems to be thriving; although it is often neglected.
 c. The rose bush seems to be thriving although it is often neglected.
 d. The rose bush seems to be thriving; although, it is often neglected.

8. Which sentence is punctuated correctly?
 a. The coupon is not valid because it expired two days ago.
 b. The coupon is not valid, because it expired two days ago.
 c. The coupon is not valid; because it expired two days ago.
 d. The coupon is not valid because, it expired two days ago.

9. Which sentence is punctuated correctly?
 a. The computers, that are in the open lab, should not be turned off after use.
 b. The computers that are in the open lab should not be turned off after use.
 c. The computers that are in the open lab, should not be turned off after use.
 d. The computers, that are in the open lab should not be turned off after use.

10. Which sentence is punctuated correctly?
 a. I want you to meet my neighbor who is a former astronaut.
 b. I want you to meet my neighbor; who is a former astronaut.
 c. I want you to meet my neighbor who, is a former astronaut.
 d. I want you to meet my neighbor, who is a former astronaut.

11. Which sentence is punctuated correctly?
 a. Passengers, who are seated in rows 25 through 30, may now board the plane.
 b. Passengers who are seated in rows 25 through 30, may now board the plane.
 c. Passengers who are seated, in rows 25 through 30, may now board the plane.
 d. Passengers who are seated in rows 25 through 30 may now board the plane.

12. Which sentence is punctuated correctly?
 a. An email from Amy reminded us of today's meeting, which is mandatory.
 b. An email from Amy reminded us of today's meeting which is mandatory.
 c. An email from Amy reminded us of today's meeting; which is mandatory.
 d. An email from Amy reminded us, of today's meeting which is mandatory.

13. Which sentence is punctuated correctly?
    a. Although we tried to keep it a secret Mike found out about his surprise party.
    b. Although we tried to keep it a secret; Mike found out about his surprise party.
    c. Although we tried to keep it a secret, Mike found out about his surprise party.
    d. Although, we tried to keep it a secret Mike found out about his surprise party.

14. Which sentence is punctuated correctly?
    a. The fields are turning brown from the drought, and there is no sign of rain.
    b. The fields are turning brown from the drought and, there is no sign of rain.
    c. The fields are turning brown from the drought; and there is no sign of rain.
    d. The fields are turning brown from the drought and there is no sign of rain.

15. Which question is structured incorrectly?
    a. A police officer asked us if we had seen a blue truck speeding in the area.
    b. Roberto asked his professor why did he have to write a research paper?
    c. Does anyone care that I have sprained my ankle?
    d. Uncle James asked Colton why he was considering joining the Marines

The Writer's World: Sentences and Paragraphs, 3rd Edition
CHAPTER 17: SENTENCE VARIETY
Summary

Chapter 17: Sentence Variety covers achieving sentence variety through varying the opening words and varying the length of sentences. The chapter opens with a Grammar Snapshot, a passage that illustrates a variety of sentence lengths.

Discussion begins with varying the opening words, such as beginning with an adverb. Examples are presented, and in Practice 1, students locate the adverb and move it to the beginning of the sentence. Beginning with a prepositional phrase is then discussed, and in Practice 2, students identify prepositional phrases in sentences and move them to the beginning of the sentence.

A hint box reminds students to use a comma after an introductory adverb or prepositional phrase. In Practice 3, students edit two passages by placing appropriate adverbs and prepositional phrases at the beginning of sentences.

Varying the length of sentences is then discussed, and an example is presented. A hint box advises students to use a comma before coordinating conjunctions that join two complete sentences. In Practice 4, students combine sentences to provide sentence variety.

In the Final Review, students are asked to edit two passages to provide sentence variety. In The Writer's Room, students are asked to write a paragraph on one of two topics presented, varying their opening words and varying the sentence length. The checklist reminds students to check for varied sentence openings and for length. In the Writer's Circle, students are asked to work with other students to create new words from the words "technological discoveries" and then to use the created words to create simple, compound, and complex sentences.

The chapter closes with a referral to MyWritingLab for further review.

CHAPTER 17: SENTENCE VARIETY AND EXACT LANGUAGE
Exercises

Set 1: Testing Concepts

1. Sentence variety means that your sentences
    a. have assorted patterns and lengths.
    b. are of generally the same length.
    c. are all short and concise.
    d. each contain a separate main idea.

2. You can vary your sentences by
    a. consciously considering the length of your sentences.
    b. altering the opening words.
    c. keeping your sentences short and concise.
    d. both a and b

3. A passage that contains only simple sentences can be
    a. interesting.
    b. complicated to interpret.
    c. boring.
    d. all of the above

4. One way to vary the opening words of a sentence is to begin with
    a. an adjective.
    b. an adverb.
    c. a pronoun.
    d. a generalization.

5. Another way to vary the opening words of a sentence is to begin with
    a. a prepositional phrase.
    b. the words *there are* or *there* is."
    c. a coordinating conjunction.
    d. the words *it is*.

6. Which of the following sentences begins with an adverb?
    a. In the end, Mia decided to join the Air Force instead of the Army.
    b. There are quite a few spelling errors in the newspaper article.
    c. Clearly, the Newark branch is in need of reorganization.
    d. La Jolla, California, is a lovely place for a vacation.

7. Which of the following sentences begins with a prepositional phrase?
    a. At the end of the road sits a charming white cottage.
    b. Despite our best efforts, we did not reach our sales goal this month.
    c. Usually, the office assistant takes notes during the meetings.
    d. It was no surprise when the expensive boutique went out of business.

8. You can vary the length of your sentences by using
    a. simple sentences.
    b. compound and complex sentences.
    c. generalizations.
    d. adverbs.

9. When you join complete sentences with coordinating conjunctions, remember to
    a. use a comma before the coordinating conjunction.
    b. use a semicolon before the coordinating conjunction.
    c. use no punctuation before the coordinating conjunction.
    d. use a period before the coordinating conjunction.

10. Which of the following words is an adverb?
    a. however
    b. therefore
    c. there
    d. periodically

11. Which of the following is a prepositional phrase?
    a. two or more
    b. before tomorrow
    c. a few hours later
    d. driving too quickly

12. Which of the following is a compound sentence?
    a. The garage sale started at 8:00 a.m., but people began arriving at 7:00 a.m.
    b. If the shoe fits, wear it.
    c. A coyote howled in the distance.
    d. Jerry stayed up late to finish his essay although he was very tired.

13. Which of the following is a complex sentence?
    a. Tomorrow, we will rise with the dawn and go fishing.
    b. An ice cold lemonade sounds refreshing, but we are out of ice cubes.
    c. Together, you and I will design our new home.
    d. Since it rained Saturday, the picnic was moved to the auditorium.

14. Which of the following is a compound-complex sentence?
    a. From the top of the Seattle Space Needle, we could see all of Seattle.
    b. My cousin is a wonderful person, but she has a tendency to talk too much.
    c. If you want my opinion, you should order a salad, but it's your decision.
    d. A sudden clap of thunder startled everyone in the room.

15. Which of the following is an adverb?
    a. unusual
    b. suddenly
    c. over
    d. except

Set 2: Testing Applications

1. Which of the following sentences begins with an adverb?
    a. Generally, the head table is served first.
    b. Through the curtains, we could see the postal carrier walking up the sidewalk.
    c. On a dare, Annie jumped off the high dive.
    d. By the time I reached the store, it had already closed.

2. Which of the following sentences begins with a prepositional phrase?
    b. When Stephanie arrives in the office, please let me know.
    a. Clearly, Ted was confused about the meeting time.
    c. In the middle of the wedding ceremony, Chad's cell phone rang.
    d. Holding his aching arm, John walked into the doctor's office.

3. Which of the following sentences begins with an adverb?
    a. On the dining room table is a package for you.
    b. Tell me, Ryan, are you planning to get a job anytime soon?
    c. Because of a minor traffic accident, traffic was backed up for blocks.
    d. Eventually, our team will win a game.

4. Which of the following sentences begins with a prepositional phrase?
    a. Unexpectedly, Stephan volunteered to chair the outreach committee.
    b. In the event of an emergency, please notify a supervisor.
    c. Four years ago, Jenny bought a condo on the beach.
    d. Although quite fattening, these cream puffs are delicious.

5. Which of the following sentences has the most variety in structure?
    a. Pedro is a hard worker, but he is often distracted.
    b. If I were you, I would try the French onion soup.
    c. Because she sang in French, I didn't understand a word, but I loved the song.
    d. The sun finally set after a long, hot day, and the construction workers were completely exhausted.

6. Which of the following sentences has the most variety in structure?
    a. Gradually, the snow subsided, and the sun shone on a sparkling white world.
    b. Sad songs are often favorites.
    c. The bookshelves in the living room need to be dusted as soon as possible.
    d. Fishing on the Deshka River is usually quite good.

7. Which of the following sentences has the most variety in structure?

    a. One of the oak trees in the back yard has fallen on the fence.

    b. Obviously, Teresa did not intentionally send that email with all her complaints to her supervisor.

    c. Finally, Brian called from London, but he didn't talk long because the rates are so high.

    d. A meeting for the reunion planning committee was held last month at Jan's house.

8. Which of the following sentences has the most variety in structure?

    a. The roses are beginning to bloom in Mrs. Carlton's garden across the street.

    b. Enrollment in college typically increases in a poor economy.

    c. Often, police officers report unusual calls during the full moon, and so do emergency room physicians.

    d. Bill called Professor Edwards' office and left a long and rambling phone message.

9. Which sentence contains an adverb that can be moved to the beginning of the sentence?

    a. There is laundry that needs to be folded.

    b. It is usually very crowded at Dave's Fish House.

    c. During business hours, employees may not use personal cell phones.

    d. Karen has been a member of a book club for several years.

10. Which sentence contains a prepositional phrase that can be moved to the beginning of the sentence?

    a. We are, unfortunately, unable to fill your order.

    b. Are you sure that these numbers are accurate?

    c. Our beloved team, the Eagles, have finally won a game.

    d. Employees had to endure construction noise for several hours.

11. Which sentence contains an adverb that can be moved to the beginning of the sentence?

    a. Beth has finally found a job that she enjoys and that pays well.

    b. Dr. Stevens charges patients $25.00 if they miss an appointment.

    c. Malcolm received a ticket on Tuesday for speeding.

    d. The temperature in the office building is too cold to be comfortable.

12. Which of the following sentences has the most variety in structure?

a. In the back of the Mr. Jensen's old barn is an antique tractor and a pile of old, rusted farm equipment.

b. Usually, the crystal bracelets sell for $45.00 because they are expensive to make, but they are now on sale for $30.00.

c. Although Jason has an impressive collection of DVDs and CDs, he is hardly ever home to enjoy them.

d. Instructions for assembling the bookshelf are clearly written in French and in German but not in English.

13. Which sentence contains a prepositional phrase that can be moved to the beginning of the sentence?

a. The chili is surprisingly easy to make.

b. Tamika has been singing at the Blue Rose Night Club for years.

c. The students were unusually subdued today.

d. Our preacher, unfortunately, has the voice of a dial tone.

14. Which sentence contains an adverb that can be moved to the beginning of the sentence?

a. The Grand Canyon, to me, is even more beautiful in the winter.

b. The ceiling fans in most homes are quite dusty.

c. It seems that children spend more time texting than watching TV.

d. The post office ordinarily closes at noon on Saturdays.

15. Which of the following sentences has the most variety in structure?

a. Undoubtedly, Cheryl will win the talent contest because her voice is beautiful, and her stage presence is impressive.

b. Everyone in our group was quite pleased with the service we received at the Mexican restaurant last evening.

c. Before starting the car, be sure that the clutch is depressed.

d. At the end of the pier is a gazebo with comfortable benches and a good shade.

The Writer's World: Sentences and Paragraphs, 3rd Edition
CHAPTER 18: FRAGMENTS
Summary

   Chapter 18: Fragments covers phrase fragments, explanatory fragments, and dependent-clause fragments. The chapter opens with a Grammar Snapshot of a passage where fragments are underlined.

   Fragments are defined as a "sentence" that lacks either a subject or verb, or it fails to express a complete thought. Phrase fragments are introduced, and examples and corrections are provided. A hint box discusses incomplete verb fragments and how to correct them. In Practice 1, students identify and correct five phrase fragments in a passage.

   Explanatory fragments are introduced next, those beginning with words such as *for example* and *such as*. Examples and correction methods are provided, and in Practice 2, students identify and correct five explanatory fragments in a passage. In Practice 3, students identify and correct five phrase and explanatory fragments in a passage.

   Dependent-clause fragments are introduced, and a chart lists common subordinating conjunctions and relative pronouns. Examples of dependent-clause fragments and their corrections are provided. In Practice 4, students identify and correct five dependent-clause fragments within a passage. In Practice 5 Review, students identify each sentence in two passages as either a fragment or a complete sentence. In Practice 6 Review, students identify and correct various types of fragments within four passages.

   In the Final Review, students edit five passages for various types of fragments. In The Writer's Room, students write about one of two topics listed and underline the sentences, ensuring each is complete. The fragment checklist reminds students to check for all types of fragments. The chapter ends with a referral to MyWritingLab for further review.

Set 1: Testing Concepts

1. A fragment is
      a. an independent clause.
      b. a compound sentence.
      c. a complete sentence.
      d. an incomplete sentence.

2. A complete sentence must
      a. have a subject.
      b. have a verb.
      c. express a complete thought.
      d. all of the above.

3. A phrase fragment is missing
      a. a subject.
      b. a verb.
      c. a subject or a verb.
      d. a subject and a verb.

4. To correct a phrase fragment,
      a. eliminate the period and connect the phrase to another sentence.
      b. connect the phrase to another sentence with a semicolon.
      c. connect the phrase to another sentence with a transition word and a semicolon.
      d. connect the phrase to another sentence with a comma and a coordinating conjunction.

5. Some phrase fragments can be corrected by adding
      a. a transition word.
      b. a helping verb.
      c. a coordinating conjunction.
      d. a period.

6. An explanatory fragment provides an explanation about a previous sentence and is missing
      a. a subject, a verb, or both.
      b. a subject.
      c. a verb.
      d. a dependent clause.

7. An explanatory fragment often begins with
    a. although.
    b. for example.
    c. however.
    d. because.

8. To correct an explanatory fragment,
    a. add the missing subject or verb.
    b. join the explanation or example to the previous sentence.
    c. replace the period with a semicolon.
    d. either a or b

9. A dependent-clause fragment has a subject and a verb,
    a. and it begins with a word like *and, but,* or *so.*
    b. and it begins with a word like *however, therefore,* or *consequently.*
    c. but it cannot stand alone.
    d. and it can stand alone.

10. To correct dependent-clause fragments,
    a. join the fragment to a complete sentence.
    b. remove the subordinating conjunction.
    c. add the necessary words in order to make it a complete idea.
    d. any of the above

11. Identify the type of fragment below.
    Especially people who spend significant time texting.
    a. a phrase fragment
    b. an explanatory fragment
    c. a dependent-clause fragment
    d. none of the above

12. Identify the type of fragment below.
    Although the forecast calls for fog.
    a. a phrase fragment
    b. an explanatory fragment
    c. a dependent-clause fragment
    d. none of the above

13. Which method would correct the sentence below?
    For instance, fresh fruits and vegetables.
    a. No changes are necessary. The sentence is complete.
    b. Connect the fragment to the previous sentence with a semicolon.
    c. Add the words *are healthful alternatives* at the end of the fragment.
    d. Remove the words *For instance.*

14. Identify the type of fragment below.

Enjoying the crisp fall air.

    a. a phrase fragment
    b. an explanatory fragment
    c. a dependent-clause fragment
    d. none of the above

15. Which method would correct the sentence below?

When we arrived at Luke's apartment.

    a. No changes are necessary. The sentence is complete.
    b. Add *last evening* to the end of the passage.
    c. Connect the fragment to the previous sentence with a semicolon.
    d. Remove the word *when*.

Set 2: Testing Applications

1. Which of the following word groups is punctuated correctly?
    a. To fix the sticking door latch. You should add some spray lubricant.
    b. To fix the sticking door latch; you should add some spray lubricant.
    c. To fix the sticking door latch, you should add some spray lubricant.
    d. To fix the sticking door latch: you should add some spray lubricant.

2. Which of the following word groups is punctuated correctly?
    a. Driving through Yellowstone Park. We saw several large elk.
    b. Driving through Yellowstone Park, we saw several large elk.
    c. Driving through Yellowstone Park; we saw several large elk.
    d. While driving through Yellowstone Park. We saw several large elk.

3. Which of the following word groups is punctuated correctly?
    a. Enchanted by the beautiful melody. I turned up the volume on the radio.
    b. Enchanted by the beautiful melody, I turned up the volume on the radio.
    c. Enchanted by the beautiful melody; I turned up the volume on the radio.
    d. Being enchanted by the beautiful melody. I turned up the volume on the radio.

4. Which of the following word groups is punctuated correctly?
    a. Martin stayed at the office until midnight. To finish the annual report.
    b. Martin stayed at the office until midnight. Finishing the annual report.
    c. Martin stayed at the office until midnight; finishing the annual report.
    d. Martin stayed at the office until midnight, finishing the annual report.

5. Which of the following word groups is punctuated correctly?
    a. Some berries are quite high in antioxidants, for example, blueberries and raspberries.
    b. Some berries are quite high in antioxidants; for example, blueberries and raspberries.
    c. Some berries are quite high in antioxidants. For example, blueberries and raspberries.
    d. Some berries are quite high in antioxidants; for example, berries such as blueberries and raspberries.

6. Which of the following word groups is punctuated correctly?
    a. The cost of the bus tour does not include extras; such as snacks and beverages.
    b. The cost of the bus tour does not include extras. Such as snacks and beverages.
    c. The cost of the bus tour does not include extras, such as snacks and beverages.
    d. The cost of the bus tour does not include extras. Items such as snacks and beverages.

7. Which of the following word groups is punctuated correctly?
   a. The smoothies come in several flavors, such as berry, banana, and orange.
   b. The smoothies come in several flavors. Such as berry, banana, and orange.
   c. The smoothies come in several flavors; such as berry, banana, and orange.
   d. The smoothies come in several flavors. And such as berry, banana, and orange.

8. Which of the following word groups is punctuated correctly?
   a. The ceremony will take place in the town square. Unless it rains.
   b. The ceremony will take place in the town square; unless it rains.
   c. The ceremony will take place in the town square: unless it rains.
   d. The ceremony will take place in the town square unless it rains.

9. Which of the following word groups is punctuated correctly?
   a. Chip is quite fond of the farm cats; although he will never admit it.
   b. Chip is quite fond of the farm cats although he will never admit it.
   c. Chip is quite fond of the farm cats. Although he will never admit it.
   d. Chip is quite fond of the farm cats. Although, he will never admit it.

10. Which of the following word groups is punctuated correctly?
   a. Since Professor Dunn is out of town. Class is cancelled tomorrow.
   b. Since Professor Dunn is out of town; class is cancelled tomorrow.
   c. Since Professor Dunn is out of town, class is cancelled tomorrow.
   d. Since Professor Dunn is out of town. So class is cancelled tomorrow.

11. Which of the following word groups is punctuated correctly?
   a. Everyone in our department was concerned about Stefan. He seemed to be under significant stress.
   b. Everyone in our department was concerned about Stefan. Because he seemed to be under significant stress.
   c. Everyone in our department was concerned about Stefan; because he seemed to be under significant stress.
   d. Everyone in our department was concerned about Stefan. Seeming to be under significant stress.

12. Which of the following word groups is punctuated correctly?
   a. The firm has hired Amanda Wilson; who has ten years' experience in management.
   b. The firm has hired Amanda Wilson, who has ten years' experience in management.
   c. The firm has hired Amanda Wilson. Who has ten years' experience in management.
   d. The firm has hired Amanda Wilson. And who has ten years' experience in management.

13. Which of the following word groups is punctuated correctly?
    a. If we can be of further assistance; please do not hesitate to call on us.
    b. If we can be of further assistance. Please do not hesitate to call on us.
    c. If we can be of further assistance, please do not hesitate to call on us.
    d. If we can be of further assistance. Do not hesitate to call on us.

14. Which of the following word groups is punctuated correctly?
    a. The road department is patching Evans Street. Which has several potholes.
    b. The road department is patching Evans Street; which has several potholes.
    c. The road department is patching Evans Street, which has several potholes.
    d. The road department is patching Evans Street. Having several potholes.

15. Which of the following word groups is punctuated correctly?
    a. You should call Thomas. Who can probably answer your question.
    b. You should call Thomas; who can probably answer your question.
    c. You should call Thomas. And who can probably answer your question.
    d. You should call Thomas, who can probably answer your question.

The Writer's World: Sentences and Paragraphs, 3rd Edition
CHAPTER 19: RUN-ONS
Summary

Chapter 19: Run-ons discusses run-on sentences and how to correct them. A Grammar Snapshot shows a paragraph with a run-on sentence highlighted in bold.

Run-on sentences are explained as complete sentences joined together without correct connecting words or punctuation. Examples of fused sentences and comma splices are provided, and a hint box advises students to look for sentences that are too long for possible run-on sentences. In Practice 1 students identify eight sentences as either correct or run-ons. Examples of how to correct run-ons are provided, and Practice 2 asks students to edit eight sentences, using various correction methods. In Practice 3, students correct eight run-on errors in two passages, using a variety of correction methods.

For the Final Review, students correct ten run-on sentences in four passages. In The Writer's Room, students write about one of two topics listed, ensuring that they do not have run-on sentences. The run-on checklist helps students check their sentences for run-ons. The chapter ends with a referral to MyWritingLab for further review.

The Writer's World: Sentences and Paragraphs, 3rd Edition
CHAPTER 19: RUN-ONS
Exercises

Set 1: Testing Concepts

1. A run-on sentence occurs when
    a. an independent clause and a dependent clause are joined incorrectly.
    b. one complete sentence is very long and rambling.
    c. two or more complete sentences are joined without correct connecting words or punctuation.
    d. two or more complete sentences are joined with a semicolon.

2. Two types of run-on sentences are
    a. a fused sentence and a comma splice.
    b. a fused sentence and a dependent clause.
    c. a comma splice and a dependent clause.
    d. a dependent clause and a phrase.

3. When two independent clauses are joined with no punctuation, the result is
    a. a comma splice.
    b. a fragment.
    c. a complex sentence.
    d. a fused sentence.

4. When two independent clauses are joined with a comma, the result is
    a. a comma splice.
    b. a fragment.
    c. a complex sentence.
    d. a fused sentence.

5. Which of the following revisions will correct a comma splice?
    a. Remove the comma between the two independent clauses.
    b. Use only a comma between two independent clauses.
    c. Remove the comma and insert a period between the two independent clauses.
    d. Use a semicolon and a coordinating conjunction between the two sentences.

6. Which of the following revisions will correct a comma splice?
    a. Use a comma followed by a conjunctive adverb and another comma between the two sentences.
    b. Use a semicolon between the two sentences.
    c. Remove all punctuation between the two sentences.
    d. Use a coordinating conjunction followed by a semicolon between the two sentences.

7. Which of the following revisions will correct a fused sentence?
   a. Use a comma followed by a coordinating conjunction between the two sentences.
   b. Use a comma followed by a conjunctive adverb between the two sentences.
   c. Remove all punctuation between the two sentences.
   d. Insert a comma between the two sentences.

8. Identify the passage that contains a comma splice.
   a. Following our yoga class, we usually enjoy smoothies at the café next door.
   b. Julie does not like flying, so she drives or takes a train when traveling.
   c. It's not an alligator, it's a crocodile.
   d. I'm looking forward to Julia Roberts' new film, which should be out soon.

9. Identify the passage that contains a fused sentence.
   a. Matt did a good job on his speech although he was nervous.
   b. Our office needs a copy machine that doesn't keep breaking.
   c. We need to leave by 1:00 p.m. to get to the airport on time.
   d. Police officers put up barricades on Lakeview Drive the road had flooded.

10. Identify the passage that contains a comma splice.
    a. If I were you, I would take Professor Williams for creative writing.
    b. The Interstate drive was enjoyable, we saw wild poppies all along the route.
    c. The outdoor play was excellent, but it was too chilly and windy to be comfortable.
    d. Because Mr. Evans will be out of town on Friday, the meeting has been postponed.

11. Identify the passage that contains a fused sentence.
    a. It was quite a surprise when Dr. Gill announced her retirement.
    b. The winner of the sweepstakes will be announced November 1st.
    c. Question 14 was tricky there seemed to be two correct answers.
    c. Has anyone seen a set of keys with a cloverleaf keychain?

12. Identify the passage that contains a comma splice.
    a. She is not a psychologist, she is a psychiatrist.
    b. The Paulsons just bought an RV, and they plan to drive to Alaska.
    c. Because your resume is impressive, we have selected you for an interview.
    d. Many people are allergic to peanuts, so they are no longer served at the bar.

13. Identify the passage that contains a fused sentence.
    a. Nobody in our family knows how to roast a turkey.
    b. We had a great time at the ball game even though our team lost.
    c. Kevin was secretly happy about the snowstorm he enjoyed the two days off work.
    d. The airport was closed because of fog, so all flights were postponed.

14. Identify the passage that contains a comma splice.
    a. Ryan is a successful architect, he designs energy-efficient homes.
    b. After seven hours on the road, we were all relieved to arrive at the hotel.
    c. Basic manicures are $25.00, and spa manicures are $40.00.
    d. When we adopted a shelter dog, our entire family became richer.

15. Identify the passage that contains a fused sentence.
    a. Someone called the office late last night but did not leave a message.
    b. I cooked the bacon and grits while the biscuits were baking in the oven.
    c. Chuck is one of those people who is always a few minutes late for work.
    d. The talking parrot was removed from the lobby customers were complaining about its foul language.

Set 2: Testing Applications

1. Choose the passage that is punctuated correctly.
   a. Maria's Coffee Shop is a good place to study it's very peaceful there.
   b. Maria's Coffee Shop is a good place to study, it's very peaceful there.
   c. Maria's Coffee Shop is a good place to study; it's very peaceful there.
   d. Maria's Coffee Shop is a good place to study; for it's very peaceful there.

2. Choose the passage that is punctuated correctly.
   a. Allan is quite a gentleman he stands up when a woman enters the room.
   b. Allan is quite a gentleman, for example, he stands up when a woman enters the room.
   c. Allan is quite a gentleman, he stands up when a woman enters the room.
   d. Allan is quite a gentleman. He stands up when a woman enters the room.

3. Choose the passage that is punctuated correctly.
   a. Roberto isn't my brother, he is my cousin.
   b. Roberto isn't my brother; he is my cousin.
   c. Roberto isn't my brother he is my cousin.
   d. Roberto isn't my brother; but he is my cousin.

4. Choose the passage that is punctuated correctly.
   a. Be sure to drink plenty of water. The temperature will reach 100 degrees today.
   b. Be sure to drink plenty of water; for the temperature will reach 100 degrees today.
   c. Be sure to drink plenty of water, the temperature will reach 100 degrees today.
   d. Be sure to drink plenty of water the temperature will reach 100 degrees today.

5. Choose the passage that is punctuated correctly.
   a. Many motorists are startled they do not expect to see camels in the pasture.
   b. Many motorists are startled, they do not expect to see camels in the pasture.
   c. Many motorists are startled; they do not expect to see camels in the pasture.
   d. Many motorists are startled; for they do not expect to see camels in the pasture.

6. Choose the passage that is punctuated correctly.
   a. Traffic is very heavy; so we will be about fifteen minutes late.
   b. Traffic is very heavy. We will be about fifteen minutes late.
   c. Traffic is very heavy, we will be about fifteen minutes late.
   d. Traffic is very heavy we will be about fifteen minutes late.

7. Choose the passage that is punctuated correctly.
   a. It was a good day in the stock market the Dow was up nearly 100 points.
   b. It was a good day in the stock market; the Dow was up nearly 100 points.
   c. It was a good day in the stock market, the Dow was up nearly 100 points.
   d. It was a good day in the stock market; because the Dow was up nearly 100 points.

8. Choose the passage that is punctuated correctly.
   a. Parents in our community are concerned; because bullying in schools is increasing.
   b. Parents in our community are concerned bullying in schools is increasing.
   c. Parents in our community are concerned, bullying in schools is increasing.
   d. Parents in our community are concerned. Bullying in schools is increasing.

9. Choose the passage that is punctuated correctly.
   a. The students were uncomfortable; the classroom was hot and stuffy.
   b. The students were uncomfortable, the classroom was hot and stuffy.
   c. The students were uncomfortable the classroom was hot and stuffy.
   d. The students were uncomfortable; for the classroom was hot and stuffy.

10. Choose the passage that is punctuated correctly.
   a. It's not the lightning that frightens our children. It's the thunder.
   b. It's not the lightning that frightens our children it's the thunder.
   c. It's not the lightning that frightens our children, it's the thunder.
   d. It's not the lightning that frightens our children; but it's the thunder.

11. Choose the passage that is punctuated correctly.
   a. The main highways will be crowded with holiday traffic; so we should take the back roads.
   b. The main highways will be crowded with holiday traffic so we should take the back roads.
   c. The main highways will be crowded with holiday traffic, so we should take the back roads.
   d. The main highways will be crowded with holiday traffic; and so we should take the back roads.

12. Choose the passage that is punctuated correctly.
   a. There was a chill in the summer air this morning soon the leaves will be turning red.
   b. There was a chill in the summer air this morning, soon the leaves will be turning red.
   c. There was a chill in the summer air this morning. Soon the leaves will be turning red.
   d. There was a chill in the summer air this morning; and soon the leaves will be turning red.

13. Choose the passage that is punctuated correctly.
   a. Michael is growing very fast, now he is taller than his father.
   b. Michael is growing very fast; now he is taller than his father.
   c. Michael is growing very fast now he is taller than his father.
   d. Michael is growing very fast; and now he is taller than his father.

14. Choose the passage that is punctuated correctly.
    a. I have lost my cell phone, I cannot find it anywhere.
    b. I have lost my cell phone I cannot find it anywhere.
    c. I have lost my cell phone; and I cannot find it anywhere.
    d. I have lost my cell phone. I cannot find it anywhere.

15. Choose the passage that is punctuated correctly.
    a. Alex needs a new truck his current one has a bad transmission.
    b. Alex needs a new truck, his current one has a bad transmission.
    c. Alex needs a new truck; his current one has a bad transmission.
    d. Alex needs a new truck; because his current one has a bad transmission.

CHAPTER 20: FAULTY PARALLEL STRUCTURE
Summary

Chapter 20: Faulty Parallel Structure covers identifying parallel structure and correcting faulty parallel structure. A Grammar Snapshot opens the chapter with a passage with parallel structures underlined.

Identifying parallel structure is explained. Examples of parallel nouns, prepositions, adjectives, and relative clauses are provided, and Practice 1 asks students to underline parallel items in eight sentences.

An explanation of how to correct faulty parallel structure is presented. Examples of corrected series of words and phrases as well as paired clauses are presented. A hint box advises students to look carefully at repeated grammatical units. In Practice 2, students edit ten sentences for errors in parallel structure.

Comparisons using comparisons with *that* or *as* is next addressed. Examples of non-parallel and parallel structures are given. Two-part constructions are also addressed: *either . . . or, not . . . but, both . . . and,* and *neither . . . nor*. In Practice 3, students revise errors in parallel structure in nine sentences. In Practice 4, students provide parallel structures for four sentences. In Practice 5 Review, students edit four sentences for errors in parallel structure.

In the Final Review, students edit five passages for errors in parallel structure. In The Writer's Room, students write about one of two topics listed, ensuring that they have no faulty parallel structures. The parallel structure checklist asks students to check their words, phrases, and clauses for parallel structure. In The Writer's Circle, students are instructed to form a team for a writing exercise in which they review their work for fragments, run-ons, and parallel structure errors. The chapter closes with a referral to MyWritingLab for further review.

Set 1: Testing Concepts

1. Parallel structure occurs when
      a. there are two central ideas in one sentence.
      b. when pairs or groups of items in a sentence are balanced.
      c. the idea in one sentence is similar to the idea in the next.
      d. none of the above

2. When you use parallel grammatical structure between words, phrases, or clauses, your
   sentences will be
      a. shorter.
      b. more confusing.
      c. more complex.
      d. clearer and smoother.

3. Parallel items in sentences can include
      a. nouns.
      b. prepositional phrases.
      c. adjectives.
      d. all of the above

4. In which of the following structures is a nonparallel structure likely to occur?
      a. in a series of words and phrases
      b. in paired clauses
      c. both a and b
      d. in transitional expressions

5. Which part of the sentence below is NOT parallel in structure?
      *On the cruise ship, classes are offered in cooking, painting, how to take
   photographs, and poker.*
      a. how to take photographs
      b. painting
      c. cooking
      d. poker

6. Which part of the sentence below is NOT parallel in structure?
      *Before riding your bicycle, check the tires, the brakes, the seat height, and
   the screws should all be tightened.*
      a. tires
      b. brakes
      c. seat height
      d. the screws should all be tightened

7. Use parallel structure when comparing or contrasting ideas using
    a. *either . . . or* constructions.
    b. *not . . . but* constructions.
    c. *neither . . . nor* constructions.
    d. all of the above

8. Choose the sentence that is NOT parallel in structure.
    a. The tea is both flavorful and light.
    b. I would rather take a multiple choice test than writing an essay.
    c. When approaching a railroad crossing, you should stop, look, and listen.
    d. The hotel is neither convenient nor inexpensive.

9. Choose the sentence that is NOT parallel in structure.
    a. Skiing requires balance, having leg strength, and some skill.
    b. Her attitude is based on either inconsideration or ignorance.
    c. At the Coffee House, courtesy is as important as promptness.
    d. An interior designer, Marianna evaluates customers' lifestyles before she designs their living spaces.

10. Choose the sentence that is NOT parallel in structure.
    a. The garden must be weeded, fertilized, and watered.
    b. According to the forest ranger, the hike is neither long nor steep.
    c. The dinner speech was both informative, and it was humorous.
    d. Steve is honest, reliable, and likable.

11. Choose the sentence that is NOT parallel in structure.
    a. There was hail damage to my car, to my motorcycle, and to the barbeque grill.
    b. Those instant lunches are neither delicious nor nutritious.
    c. Shane would much rather fly to New York than driving his car.
    d. We spent much of the day vacuuming the carpets and waxing the floors.

12. Choose the sentence that is NOT parallel in structure.
    a. In police work, observation skills are as important as listening skills.
    b. I would rather watch a DVD at home than going to a crowded theater.
    c. The new motorcycle model is both fast and sleek.
    d. Taking a photograph is somewhat like painting a scene.

13. Choose the sentence that is NOT parallel in structure.
    a. Aunt Beth would rather play tennis than watching a match on television.
    b. My job duties include making coffee, preparing salads, and stocking shelves.
    c. Tourists evacuated the park as firefighters rushed in to battle the fire.
    d. We found that the resort was neither crowded nor overpriced.

14. Choose the sentence that is NOT parallel in structure.
   a. We spent our vacation days shopping, dining, and playing golf.
   b. The stock market seems to be up one day and down the next.
   c. You can either carry your briefcase on the plane or check it as baggage.
   d. Unfortunately, Pete can neither sing on key nor remembering the words.

15. Choose the sentence that is NOT parallel in structure.
   a. After the long flight to New Zealand, Keith was both tired and irritable.
   b. The department store is clean and well-stocked.
   c. Victoria would rather study a little each day than cram right before an exam.
   d. The newspaper article is not only biased, but it also has inaccuracies.

Set 2: Testing Applications

1. Which sentence is parallel in structure?
a. By the end of the class period, the students were confused, and they felt overwhelmed.
   b. By the end of the class period, the students were confused and overwhelmed.
   c. By the end of the class period, the students felt confused and they were overwhelmed.
d. By the end of the class period, the students felt confused, and the material was overwhelming.

2. Which sentence is parallel in structure?
a. Adult leisure classes are being offered in painting, journaling, and how to make jewelry.
   b. Adult leisure classes are being offered in painting techniques, how to journal, and jewelry making.
c. Adult leisure classes are being offered in how to paint, how to journal, and jewelry making.
   d. Adult leisure classes are being offered in painting, journaling, and jewelry making.

3. Which sentence is parallel in structure?
   a. It was not only miserably hot, but it was humid.
   b. It was not only miserably hot, it was also humid.
   c. It was not only miserably hot, but it was also humid.
   d. It was not only miserably hot, but the humidity was high.

4. Which sentence is parallel in structure?
   a. The restaurant's salmon was neither substandard, nor was it impressive.
   b. The restaurant's salmon was neither substandard nor impressive.
   c. The restaurant's salmon was not substandard nor did it impress me.
   d. The restaurant's salmon was not substandard nor an impressive meal.

5. Which sentence is parallel in structure?
   a. We don't need more complaints; we need more solutions.
   b. We don't need more complaints; solutions are what we need.
   c. We don't need more complaining; we need more solutions.
   d. We don't need more complaining; solutions are what we need.

6. Which sentence is parallel in structure?
   a. Jen wants a car that is compact yet having roominess.
   b. Jen wants a car that is compact yet has roominess.
   c. Jen wants a car that is compact yet roomy.
   d. Jen wants a car that has compactness yet having roominess.

7. Which sentence is parallel in structure?
    a. As a supervisor, Miguel is more decisive and motivating than John.
    b. As a supervisor, Miguel can make decisions better and is more motivating than John.
    c. As a supervisor, Miguel can make decisions more quickly and is a better motivator than John.
    d. As a supervisor, Miguel is more decisive and a better motivator than John.

8. Which sentence is parallel in structure?
    a. You can bring your own lunch to work, or catered lunches are available.
    b. You can bring your own lunch to work, or a catered lunch can be purchased.
    c. Your own lunch can be brought to work or purchase a catered lunch.
    d. You can bring your own lunch to work or purchase a catered lunch.

9. Which sentence is parallel in structure?
    a. Her latest novel is fast-paced, romantic, and it has humor.
    b. Her latest novel has a fast pace, romance, and is humorous.
    c. Her latest novel is fast-paced, romantic, and humorous.
    d. Her latest novel has a fast pace, romance, and humorous.

10. Which sentence is parallel in structure?
    a. So far, my cooking course is not interesting nor useful.
    b. So far, my cooking course is neither interesting nor useful.
    c. So far, my cooking course is not interesting and useless.
    d. So far, my cooking course is neither interesting nor of use.

11. Which sentence is parallel in structure?
    a. Ellen is a pilot who is skilled but cautious.
    b. Ellen is a pilot who has good skills but cautious.
    c. Ellen is a pilot who is skilled but uses caution.
    d. Ellen is a pilot who has good skills but is cautious.

12. Which sentence is parallel in nature?
    a. During our flight, we endured rowdy teens beside us and a screaming child behind us.
    b. During our flight, we endured rowdy teens beside us and a child was screaming behind us.
    c. During our flight, we endured teens that were rowdy beside us and a screaming child behind us.
    d. During our flight, we endured teens that were rowdy beside us and a child was screaming behind us.

13. Which sentence is parallel in structure?
    a. The defendant's story was not only unbelievable but it was ridiculous.
    b. The defendant's story was not only not believable, but ridiculous.
    c. The defendant's story was not only not believable, but ridiculousness.
    d. The defendant's story was not only unbelievable, but it was also ridiculous.

14. Which sentence is parallel in structure?
      a. We kept the kitten because she is loving, playful, and she behaves.
      b. We kept the kitten because she is loving, plays, and well-behaved.
      c. We kept the kitten because she is loving, playful, and well-behaved.
      d. We kept the kitten because she is loving, a playful kitten, and she behaves.

15. Which sentence is parallel in structure?
      a. There are only two choices at the theater, a romance or a funny movie.
      b. There are only two choices at the theater, a romance or a comedy.
      c. There are only two choices at the theater, a romantic movie or a comedy.
      d. There are only two choices at the theater, a romantic movie or one that is funny.

The Writer's World: Sentences and Paragraphs, 3rd Edition
CHAPTER 21: ADJECTIVES AND ADVERBS
Summary

Chapter 21: Adjectives and Adverbs covers general adjectives and adverbs as well as comparative and superlative forms. The chapter opens with a Grammar Snapshot, a passage in which adjectives and adverbs are underlined.

Adjectives are defined and underlined in three example sentences. In Practice 1, students identify adjectives in five sentences. The placement of adjectives, either before a noun or after a linking verb, is discussed. A hint box points out the difference between the placement of adjectives in English versus other languages. In Practice 2, students correct errors in adjective placement in five sentences. The order of adjectives is also discussed, and a hint box discusses the use of commas between adjectives of equal weight. In Practice 3, students fill in adjectives in the correct order in three passages.

Problems with adjectives are discussed, specifically, the spelling of adjectives ending in *–ful* or *–less* and those that look like verbs because of *–ing* or *–ed* endings. A hint box advises students to keep adjectives in the singular form. In Practice 4, students correct nine adjective errors in two passages.

Adverbs are discussed next and are described as words that add information to adjectives, verbs, and other adverbs. Examples are provided, and special note is made of the common *–ly* ending for many adverbs. A hint box discusses those adverbs and adjectives that have the same form. In Practice 5, students change ten adjectives to adverbs.

Placement of frequency adverbs is discussed, with examples, and Practice 6 asks students to correct six errors in word order or adjective and adverb forms. Students are cautioned to avoid using an adjective instead of an adverb after a verb. In Practice 7, students edit eight sentences for errors in adverb or adjective forms or placement.

Special note is made of *good* and *well*, and *bad* and *badly*. Examples of correct usage are provided, and Practice 8 asks students to identify the correct adjective or adverb in five short passages.

Comparative and superlative forms are addressed. Students are instructed to use the comparative form to compare two items and the superlative form to compare three or more items. Examples are provided, and hints are provided for remembering these forms. A hint box discusses the difference between *farther* and *further*. In Practice 9, students write the comparative and superlative forms of twelve adjectives and adverbs. Practice 10 asks students to identify the correct comparative or superlative form of adjectives or adverbs in ten sentences. In Practice 11, students provide the correct comparative or superlative form for the adjectives in three passages.

Problems with comparative and superlative forms are also discussed, specifically not using *more* and *–er* to modify the same word. Examples are provided, and a hint box explains *the more . . . the better* construction. In Practice 12, students correct ten adjective and adverb errors in four passages.

In the Final Review, students edit five passages for errors with adjectives and adverbs. In The Writer's Room, students write about one of two listed topics and then identify their adjectives and adverbs. An adjective and adverb checklist reminds students to check for the correct placement, order, and spelling of adjectives and adverbs. The chapter closes with a referral to MyWritingLab for further review.

Set 1: Testing Concepts

1. Adjectives describe
    a. nouns and pronouns.
    b. verbs.
    c. adverbs.
    d. prepositions.

2. Which of the following questions does an adjective answer?
    a. How?
    b. When?
    c. What kind?
    d. Where?

3. Which of the following questions does an adjective answer?
    a. Which one?
    b. How many?
    c. Whose?
    d. all of the above

4. Identify the adjective in the sentence below:
    During the night, a thick layer of fog settled over the town.
    a. During
    b. thick
    c. fog
    d. settled

5. Identify the adjective in the sentence below:
    Brittany's plane stopped unexpectedly in Chicago.
    a. Brittany's
    b. plane
    c. unexpectedly
    d. in

6. Adjectives can be placed either before a noun or
    a. before a verb.
    b. after an action verb.
    c. before a conjunction.
    d. after a linking verb.

7. When placing two or more adjectives together, use the following order:
   a. color, number, size, quality, age, origin, and type.
   b. origin, number, age, quality, size, type, and color.
   c. number, quality, size, age, color, origin, and type.
   d. size, quality, age, origin, type, color, and number.

8. Adverbs add information to
   a. verbs.
   b. verbs, adjectives, and other adverbs.
   c. nouns and pronouns.
   d. verbs and adjectives.

9. Adverbs answer all of the following questions except
   a. How?
   b. Whose?
   c. When?
   d. Where?

10. Adverbs often end in
    a. *–d* or *–ed*.
    b. *–ful*.
    c. *–ness*.
    d. *–ly*.

11. Frequency adverbs, such as *always, often, sometimes, usually,* or *ever* are placed
    a. before regular present- and past-tense verbs.
    b. after the verb *be*.
    c. after helping verbs.
    d. all of the above.

12. What is the adverb form of *good*?
    a. better
    b. well
    c. best
    d. both b and c

13. To compare two items, use
    a. the comparative form of the adjective.
    b. the superlative form of the adjective.
    c. the base form of the adjective.
    d. the *–est* form of the adjective.

14. To compare three or more items, use
    a. the comparative form of the adjective.
    b. the superlative form of the adjective.
    c. the base form of the adjective.
    d. the *–er* form of the adjective.

15. When you compare most adjectives and adverbs of two or more syllables, add
_____ .
    a. *–er* or *–est*
    b. *–d* or *–ed*
    c. *more* or *the most*
    d. none of the above

Set 2: Testing Applications

1. Identify the adjective in the following sentence:
   Shanna awoke in the morning with a dry cough.
   a. Shanna
   b. awoke
   c. with
   d. dry

2. Which sentence reflects the correct order of adjectives?
   a. Linda received twelve red bright roses for her birthday.
   b. Linda received bright red twelve roses for her birthday.
   c. Linda received twelve bright red roses for her birthday.
   d. Linda received roses twelve bright red for her birthday.

3. Which sentence reflects the correct use of adjectives?
   a. The moon is shining more brighter tonight than usual.
   b. We hesitantly entered the noisy restaurant.
   c. The tornado was a terrified experience for Jason.
   d. Jack endured a very bored commencement speech.

4. Identify the adverb in the sentence below.
   During dinner, a mixture of rain and snow fell steadily.
   a. steadily
   b. fell
   c. mixture
   d. during

5. Choose the sentence in which the adverbs are used correctly.
   a. I did not do good on the midterm, but Jessica did a well job.
   b. I did not do well on the midterm, but Jessica did a well job.
   c. I did not do good on the midterm, but Jessica did a good job.
   d. I did not do well on the midterm, but Jessica did a good job.

6. Choose the sentence in which the modifier is used correctly.
   a. The team's defense should play more aggressive.
   b. I apologized sincerely for forgetting Lisa's birthday.
   c. Amanda did real well on her algebra exam.
   d. The flood waters were rising steady.

7. Choose the sentence in which the modifier is used correctly.
   a. During her audition, Victoria sang good.
   b. Jerome felt badly about wrecking his father's car.
   c. Don't feel bad about missing the meeting.
   d. The Eagles played good in the second half of the game.

8. Choose the sentence in which the modifier is used correctly.
   a. White wine generally goes well with seafood.
   b. Myra has a bad headache and does not feel good.
   c. After being painted, our house looks well.
   d. The basketball team does not shoot free throws good.

9. Choose the sentence in which the modifier is used correctly.
   a. Damian goes to Hawaii quite regular.
   b. My new cell phone has more better coverage than my old one.
   c. Yesterday was the most happiest day of my life.
   d. Jill works more effectively alone than in a group.

10. Choose the sentence in which the modifier is used correctly.
    a. Coach Nelson felt badly that he had to bench the star forward.
    b. I can't believe how bad I did during the job interview.
    c. The manager did not seem to feel bad about firing Leslie.
    d. No one in the class did good on the comma quiz.

11. Choose the sentence in which the modifier is used correctly.
    a. The Hawaiian coffee tastes more smoother than the Costa Rican coffee.
    b. If you need farther assistance, please call us.
    c. Driving the tractor is more easier than driving a truck.
    d. The website instructions are more helpful than those in the pamphlet.

12. Choose the sentence in which the modifier is used correctly.
    a. Running on hard pavement is really hard on Brandon's knees.
    b. After gardening for two hours, we were sure ready for a break.
    c. It sure is hot and muggy today.
    d. Meredith believes very strong in daily exercise and meditation.

13. Choose the sentence in which the modifier is used correctly.
    a. Getting a pet alligator was not one of Tim's better ideas.
    b. Between tennis and badminton, I like tennis better.
    c. Of all the people in the office, Marcus is the best writer.
    d. Of the twins. Kaylee is the tallest.

14. Choose the sentence in which the modifier is used correctly.
    a. You shouldn't feel too badly about losing my book; I have another copy.
    b. Jewel is one of the better singers currently on tour.
    c. Jennifer Gray did good on *Dancing with the Stars.*
    d. Of the triplets, Carly has the best GPA.

15. Choose the sentence in which the modifier is used correctly.
    a. We must talk real quietly in this library.
    b. Dennis is quite a bit more taller than his brother.
    c. It's surely humid outside, isn't it?
    d. My new computer is definitely more faster than my old one.

Chapter 22: Mistakes with Modifiers covers misplaced and dangling modifiers. The chapter opens with a Grammar Snapshot of a passage with modifiers underlined.

Misplaced modifiers are described as words, phrases, or clauses that are not placed next to the word or words that they want to modify. Examples of misplaced modifiers are provided, along with their corrections.

Common misplaced modifiers are discussed, beginning with prepositional phrase modifiers. Examples are provided, and Practice 1 asks students to identify prepositional phrase modifiers in five sentences and then draw an arrow to the words they modify. Present participle modifiers are explained, with examples of unclear and corrected modifiers. Practice 2 asks students to identify present participle modifiers in five sentences and then draw an arrow from the modifiers to the words they modify. Past participle modifiers are explained, with examples, and Practice 3 asks students to identify past participle modifiers in five sentences and then draw arrows from the modifiers to the words they modify. Finally, other dependent-clause modifiers are addressed, and examples are provided. In Practice 4, students identify relative clause modifiers and then draw arrows from the modifiers to the words they modify. In Practice 5, students identify sentences that use modifiers correctly. A hint box describes three ways to correct misplaced modifiers. In Practice 6, students edit eight sentences for misplaced modifiers.

Dangling modifiers are explained as modifiers that open a sentence but do not modify any words in the sentence. Examples and corrections are provided, and in Practice 7, students identify the correctly structured sentences in six pairs of sentences. A hint box shows three ways to correct dangling modifiers. In Practice 8, students correct dangling modifiers by rewriting five sentences. In Practice 9, students edit seven sentences for misplaced and dangling modifiers.

In the Final Review, students edit three passages for errors with modifiers. In The Writer's Room, students write about one of three listed topics and take care to avoid misplaced and dangling modifiers. A modifier checklist lists types of misplaced and dangling modifiers to check for. The Writer's Circle instructs students to work in a group to write a paragraph that has no misplaced or dangling modifiers. The chapter ends with a referral to MyWritingLab for supplemental review.

The Writer's World: Sentences and Paragraphs, 3rd Edition
CHAPTER 22: MISTAKES WITH MODIFIERS
Exercises

Set 1: Testing Concepts

1. A modifier is a word, phrase, or a clause that
    a. provides a transition from one sentence to another.
    b. introduces an independent clause.
    c. describes or modifies nouns or verbs in a sentence.
    d. all of the above

2. To use a modifier correctly, it must be placed
    a. next to the word or words that you want to modify.
    b. before the verb.
    c. after the verb.
    d. before the subject.

3. A word, phrase, or clause that is not placed next to the word that it is intended to
   modify is called
    a. a parallel structure error.
    b. a fragment.
    c. a misplaced modifier.
    d. a dangling modifier.

4. A prepositional phrase modifier
    a. is made of a prepositional phrase and its object.
    b. is made of a phrase that begins with a past participle.
    c. can begin with a subordinator or a relative pronoun.
    d. is made of a phrase that begins with an –*ing* verb.

5. In the sentence below, identify the prepositional phrase modifier.
        Last night I played Monopoly with my two nieces.
    a. Last night
    b. I played
    c. Monopoly
    d. with my two nieces

6. In the sentence below, identify the word being modified by the prepositional phrase.
        Derek ordered a cheeseburger with extra fries.
    a. Derek
    b. ordered
    c. cheeseburger
    d. extra

7. In the sentence below, identify the present participle modifier.

    Laura's son is the quarterback wearing number five.

    a. Laura's

    b. son

    c. quarterback

    d. wearing number five

8. In the sentence below, identify the word being modified.

    Laura's son is the quarterback wearing number five.

    a. Laura's

    b. number

    c. quarterback

    d. is

9. In the sentence below, identify the past participle modifier.

    Worried about his job security, Blake started working longer hours.

    a. Worried about his job security

    b. Blake

    c. started working

    d. longer hours.

10. In the sentence below, identify the word being modified.

    Worried about his job security, Blake started working longer hours.

    a. Worried

    b. Blake

    c. security

    d. working

11. A modifier that opens a sentence but does not modify any words in the sentence is called

    a. a misplaced modifier.

    b. a dangling modifier.

    b. a fragment.

    d. faulty agreement.

12. To correct a misplaced modifier,

    a. add a subordinator.

    b. add a coordinator.

    c. move the modifier next to the word(s) being modified.

    d. make sure that the modifier and the first noun following it have a logical connection.

13. To correct a dangling modifier,

    a. add a subordinator.

    b. add a coordinator.

    c. move the modifier next to the word(s) being modified.

    d. make sure that the modifier and the first noun following it have a logical connection.

14. Which sentence contains a dangling modifier?

    a. Excited about the upcoming cruise, Danielle began packing early.

    b. Entering the grocery store, a spilled drink caused Jeff to trip and fall.

    c. While cooking supper, I had to answer my cell phone three times.

    d. To learn more about cholesterol, David did a search on the internet.

15. Which sentence contains a dangling modifier?

    a. While watching television, the power suddenly went out.

    b. To turn off the computer, you should push the green button.

    c. Bored with her job at the restaurant, Tonya decided to return to college.

    d. Dreaming of a great fortune, Marvin bought a lottery ticket.

Set 2: Testing Applications

1. Which sentence contains a misplaced modifier?
    a. Talking on my cell phone, my cat kept interrupting me.
    b. While waiting at a red light, I listened to my favorite song on the radio.
    c. On Wednesday, the stock market fell over 100 points.
    d. We admired Clair's photograph of a swan in a lake.

2. Which sentence contains a dangling modifier?
    a. To open the gas tank door, pull the handle to the left of the driver's seat.
    b. While flying from Boston to Denver, Bill had a layover in Atlanta.
    c. We admired a photograph of the Grand Canyon hanging on the wall.
    d. Delighted with the cuddly teddy bear, I bought one for my niece.

3. Which sentence contains a misplaced modifier?
    a. Can you see that cloud shaped like a dog?
    b. I bought an apple at the grocery store that cost only fifty cents.
    c. The pizza can be ordered with any of three toppings.
    d. In just two weeks, Kevin's new car will arrive at the dealership.

4. Which sentence contains a dangling modifier?
    a. To our surprise, a foot of snow fell during the night.
    b. After traveling for two weeks, we were quite exhausted.
    c. Thinking about a new computer, Jared did some research on the Internet.
    d. To get a good seat at the concert, tickets must be purchased in advance.

5. Choose the sentence that is structured correctly.
    a. Wanting an A in algebra, getting a tutor seemed like the best option for Ed.
    b. Wanting an A in algebra, Ed's plan was to get a tutor.
    c. Wanting an A in algebra, Ed decided to get a tutor.
    d. Ed's best option was to get a tutor, wanting an A in algebra.

6. Choose the sentence that is structured correctly.
    a. Near Wichita, Micah bought a small farmhouse, which needs a new coat of paint.
    b. Micah bought a small farmhouse near Wichita, which needs a new coat of paint.
    c. Needing a new coat of paint, Micah bought a small farmhouse near Wichita.
    d. Near Wichita, needing a new coat of pain, Micah bought a small farmhouse.

7. Choose the sentence that is structured correctly.
    a. Hoping to arrive at my aunt's house before dark, I took the bypass around Atlanta.
    b. Taking the bypass around Atlanta, my plan was to arrive at my aunt's house before dark.

c. Hoping to arrive at my aunt's house before dark, the bypass around Atlanta seemed like the best plan.

d. Taking the bypass around Atlanta, arriving at my aunt's house before dark seemed possible.

8. Choose the sentence that is structured correctly.

a. Set by an arsonist in the morning newspaper, I read that a grass fire was doused by firefighters.

b. I read in the morning newspaper that a grass fire was doused by firefighters set by an arsonist.

c. Set by an arsonist, I read in the morning newspaper that firefighters had doused a grass fire.

d. In the morning newspaper, I read that firefighters doused a grass fire set by an arsonist.

9. Choose the sentence that is structured correctly.

a. An elderly man was convicted of disorderly conduct during a fit of rage by the jury.

a. An elderly man was convicted of disorderly conduct by the jury during a fit of rage.

c. A jury convicted an elderly man of disorderly conduct during a fit of rage.

b. During a fit of rage, a jury convicted an elderly man of disorderly conduct.

10. Choose the sentence that is structured correctly.

a. While sipping coffee at a coffee shop, Jack's car rolled into the street.

b. While he was sipping coffee at a coffee shop, Jack's car rolled into the street.

c. Sipping coffee at the local coffee shop, Jack's car rolled into the street.

d. Sipping coffee at the local coffee shop, into the street rolled Jack's car.

11. Choose the sentence that is structured correctly.

a. I found my wallet containing all my credit cards lying on the ground beside my car.

b. Lying on the ground beside my car, I found my wallet containing all my credit cards.

c. Lying beside my car on the ground, I found my wallet containing all my credit cards.

d. I found my wallet on the ground beside my car containing all my credit cards.

12. Choose the sentence that is structured correctly.

a. Driving into Las Vegas, the dazzling lights delighted Dave.

b. Driving into Las Vegas, the dazzling lights were delightful to Dave.

c. Driving into Las Vegas, Dave was delighted by the dazzling lights.

d. The dazzling lights, driving into Las Vegas, were delightful to Dave.

13. Choose the sentence that is structured correctly.

    a. To receive a refund, the computer must be returned within thirty days.

    b. To receive a refund, you must return the computer within thirty days.

    c. The computer, to receive a refund, must be returned within thirty days.

    d. In order to receive a refund, the computer must be returned within thirty days.

14. Which sentence is structured correctly?

    a. At a press conference, it was revealed that the Eastside Bank had been robbed by the chief of police.

    b. It was revealed at a press conference that the Eastside Bank had been robbed by the chief of police.

    c. The chief of police revealed that the Eastside Bank had been robbed at a press conference.

    d. At a press conference, the chief of police revealed that the Eastside Bank had been robbed.

15. Which sentence is structured correctly?

    a. During the class lecture, the essays were called the worst batch ever written by Professor Wyatt.

    b. During the class lecture, Professor Wyatt called the essays by worst batch ever written.

    c. Professor Wyatt called the essays the worst batch ever written during the class lecture.

    d. According to Professor Wyatt, the essays were the worst batch ever written during a class lecture.

The Writer's World: Sentences and Paragraphs, 3rd Edition
CHAPTER 23: EXACT LANGUAGE

Summary

Chapter 23: Exact Language covers using a dictionary and thesaurus, using specific vocabulary, avoiding clichés, and slang versus Standard American English. The chapter opens with a Grammar Snapshot that demonstrates descriptive language.

Using a dictionary and thesaurus is introduced. Covered in the dictionary section are the preface, notes, prefixes, part of speech, and word division. A hint box explains cognates. In Practice 1, Part A, students find abbreviation keys for parts of speech and record them. In Part B, students write definitions and the part of speech for four words.

A hint box explains stressed syllables in online dictionaries and thesauruses. In Practice 2, students look up ten words to find the stressed syllable.

The thesaurus is discussed next and recommended to avoid repeating the same word. In Practice 3, students use a thesaurus to find at least five synonyms for five words.

Using specific vocabulary is addressed, and a list of vague words with more precise words is presented. How to create vivid language is discussed, and examples are provided. In Practice 4, students underline vivid words in a passage. In Practice 5, students replace vague words with more precise or vivid details in five sentences.

The next section discusses avoiding clichés. A list of common clichés and possible solutions is presented. In Practice 6, students identify and replace vague words in eight sentences.

Slang versus Standard American English is then addressed. Examples and corrections are provided, and in Practice 7, students change slang to Standard American English in ten sentences.

In the Final Review, students edit four passages for clichés and slang expressions. In The Writer's Room, students choose one of two topics presented and write a paragraph, ensuring that their sentences use exact language. A checklist reminds students to edit their work for clear and specific vocabulary. The chapter ends with a referral to MyWritingLab for further review.

Set 1: Concepts

1. In addition to a word's meaning, a dictionary also provides information about
     a. the part of speech.
     b. pronunciation.
     c. the word's history.
     d. all of the above

2. Explanations about the various symbols and abbreviations in the dictionary can be found
     a. in the dictionary's index.
     b. in the dictionary's table of contents.
     c. in the dictionary's preface.
     d. at the bottom of each page in the dictionary.

3. If you are looking up a word that has a prefix such as *un-* or *mis-*, you may have to
     a. look up the root word.
     b. look in a larger dictionary.
     c. look up the word in Latin.
     d. check Wikipedia.

4. Dots between letters in a word in a dictionary entry indicate
     a. where the word is stressed.
     b. word break divisions.
     c. prefixes
     d. suffixes

5. English words that may look and sound like words in another language are called
     a. syllables
     b. cognates
     c. root words
     d. prefixes

6. To avoid using the same word over and over in writing, use
     a. an encyclopedia.
     b. a dictionary.
     c. a spell checker.
     d. a thesaurus.

7. A word that is similar to another but not exact in meaning is
    a. a thesaurus.
    b. a cognate.
    c. a synonym.
    d. an antonym.

8. A nuance means
    a. a shade of meaning.
    b. the opposite meaning.
    c. a word choice error.
    d. a descriptive word.

9. When you write, you should replace vague words with
    a. generalizations.
    b. specific words.
    c. clichés.
    d. sophisticated words.

10. To convey your meaning exactly, choose words that are
    a. clichés.
    b. generalizations.
    c. vague.
    d. vivid and precise.

11. An expression that is overused is called
    a. a cognate.
    b. a synonym.
    c. a cliché.
    d. a nuance.

12. Which of the following expressions is common and overused?
    a. in the blink of an eye
    b. as slick as a new deck of cards
    c. as quiet as an eye blink
    d. a body shaped like a pear

13. The language generally used and expected in schools, businesses, and government institutions is called
    a. English.
    b. Standard American English.
    c. the King's English.
    d. slang.

171

14. Slang should be used in
   a. academic essays.
   b. business letters.
   c. government documents.
   d. informal situations.

15. Which of the following expressions is considered slang?
   a. intoxicated
   b. inebriated
   c. smashed
   d. under the influence

Set 2: Application

1. Which of the following is the most specific?
   a. a flower
   b. a vegetable
   c. a tree
   d. a dandelion

2. Which of the following is the most specific?
   a. a beautiful sunset
   b. a stunning sunset
   c. a pink and orange sunset
   d. a colorful sunset

3. Which of the following is the most specific?
   a. whispered
   b. stated
   c. said
   d. talked

4. Which of the following is the most specific?
   a. an employee
   b. a forest ranger
   c. a public servant
   d. an American

5. Which of the following descriptions is the most vivid and specific?
   a. a flock of birds
   b. a straight highway
   c. a coal black kitten with green eyes
   d. an interesting book of short stories

6. Which of the following descriptions is the most vivid and specific?
   a. trees blowing in a brisk wind
   b. a very friendly and excited dog
   c. a very serious traffic accident at an intersection
   d. bare oak trees silhouetted against an orange sky

7. Which of the following statements does NOT contain a cliché?
   a. He trudged slowly toward his car.
   b. She is as busy as a bee.
   c. Matt wants to be top dog.
   d. I enjoy spending quality time with my family.

8. Which of the following statements does NOT contain a cliché?
   a. It was so dark I couldn't see my hand in front of my face.
   b. Last but not least, we would like to honor Bev.
   c. The police arrived in the nick of time.
   d. My computer seems to be sluggish today.

9. Which of the following statements does NOT contain a cliché?
   a. It's easier said than done.
   b. Are you working hard or hardly working?
   c. You deserved that promotion.
   d. I will finish this project, slowly but surely.

10. Which of the following statements does NOT contain a cliché?
    a. She is certainly in for a rude awakening.
    b. You were fortunate to have found that error.
    c. Ben has a chip on his shoulder.
    d. It's raining cats and dogs outside.

11. Which of the following is the most appropriate expression for academic and business writing?
    a. This cash register is freaking me out.
    b. This cash register is making me crazy.
    c. This cash register is making me frustrated.
    d. This cash register is possessed.

12. Which of the following is the most appropriate expression for academic and business writing?
    a. When the quarterback threw an interception, Ben lost his temper.
    b. When the quarterback threw an interception. Ben had a meltdown.
    c. When the quarterback threw an interception, Ben blew his top.
    d. When the quarterback threw an interception, Ben flipped out.

13. Which of the following is the most appropriate expression for academic and business writing?
    a. There's a ginormous sale at the shoe boutique.
    b. There's a big sale at the shoe boutique.
    c. There's a big time sale at the shoe boutique.
    d. There's a monster sale at the shoe boutique.

14. Which of the following is the most appropriate expression for academic and business writing?

        a. I like hanging with my friends.
        b. Wendy needs to chill out.
        c. That cat's stare is creeping me out.
        d. The mayor seemed distracted at the press conference.

15. Which of the following is the most appropriate expression for academic and business writing?

        a. Kyle made us an amazing pizza last night.
        b. We all stuffed our faces on Kyle's pizza.
        c. Kyle has a special recipe for his pizza dough.
        d. After pizza, we all just hung out.

Summary

Chapter 24: Spelling, covers improving spelling, rules for *ie* or *ei,* adding prefixes and suffixes, writing two-part words, and commonly misspelled words. The chapter opens with a Grammar Snapshot, a paragraph in which commonly misspelled words are underlined.

Instruction begins with how to improve spelling. A hint box reminds students of the difference between vowels and consonants. In Practice 1, students write words with various vowel and consonant combinations.

Words with *ie* or *ei* combinations are discussed, and rules are explained, with examples. Practice 2 asks students to identify the correct spelling of twelve words with *ie* or *ei* combinations. In Practice 3, students edit sentences for spelling errors.

Adding prefixes and suffixes is addressed next. Rules and examples for prefixes and suffices are presented, and a hint box addresses words ending in *–ful*. In Practice 4, students identify the correct spelling of fourteen pairs of words. Adding *–s* or *–es* suffixes is discussed, and examples and exceptions are listed. In Practice 5, students add *–s* or *–es* to twelve words. Rules for adding suffixes to words ending in *–e* are also addressed, with examples and exceptions listed. In Practice 6, students rewrite ten words by adding suggested endings. In Practice 7, students correct spelling errors in three passages.

Adding suffixes by doubling the final consonant is introduced, and rules and exceptions are listed. Practice 8 asks students to rewrite ten words with suggested endings. The last rule in this section addresses adding suffixes to words ending in *–y.* Examples and exceptions are listed, and in Practice 9, students rewrite ten words by adding suggested endings. In Practice 10, students edit two passages for spelling errors.

Writing two-part words is introduced, and a hint box focuses on *another* and *a lot.* In Practice 11, students edit a paragraph for spelling errors.

A list of 120 commonly misspelled words is presented, and a hint box cautions students that spelling checkers on word processors are not always accurate. In Practice 12, students edit four passages for spelling errors. A hint box advises students to keep a spelling log, to use memory cards, to write down difficult words, and to check a dictionary to verify the spelling of difficult words.

In the Final Review, students edit four passages for spelling errors. In The Writer's Room, students write about one of two topics listed and circle any words that they have misspelled. The spelling rules checklist reminds students of spelling rules so that they can check their spelling. The chapter ends with a referral to MyWritingLab for more review.

CHAPTER 24: SPELLING
Exercises

Set 1: Testing Concepts

1. Spelling mistakes
      a. are generally not very noticeable in business writing.
      b. can detract from good ideas in your writing.
      c. are generally not important in most writing situations.
      d. all of the above

2. You can be a better speller if you
      a. guess at words that you do not know how to spell.
      b. rely on your word processor's spell checker.
      c. proofread your written work and check a dictionary for the meaning and spelling of words.
      d. all of the above

3. The letters *a, e, i, o, u* and sometimes *y* are considered
      a. vowels.
      b. suffixes.
      c. consonants.
      d. prefixes.

4. All letters except *a, e, i, o, u* and sometimes *y* are considered
      a. suffixes.
      b. vowels.
      c. consonants.
      d. prefixes.

5. When spelling a word containing *–ie* or *–ei*, such as *receive*,
      a. write *–e* before *–i*, always.
      b. write *–e* before *–i*, except after *–c* or when *–ei* is pronounced as *–ay*, as in *neighbor* and *weigh*.
      c. write *–i* before *–e*, always.
      d. write *–i* before *–e*, except after *–c* or when *–ei* is pronounced as *–ay*, as in *neighbor* and *weigh*.

6. When you add a prefix to a word, such as *un + natural*,
      a. keep the last letter of the prefix, but eliminate the first letter of the main word.
      b. keep the last letter of the prefix and the first letter of the main word.
      c. add a hyphen between the prefix and the word.
      d. keeping the last letter of the prefix is optional.

7. When you add the suffix –ly to word that ends in –l, such as *beautiful*,
    a. the extra –l is optional.
    b. eliminate one –l.
    c. keep the –l of the root word.
    d. change the –y to –i and add –ies.

8. To form the plural of words that end in –s, –sh, –ss, –ch, or –x, such as *birch*,
    a. add –es.
    b. add -s.
    c. add –ies.
    d. add –en.

9. To form the plural of words that end in the consonant –y, such as *poppy*,
    a. add –ies.
    b. simply add an –s.
    c. add –s or –es.
    d. change the –y to –i and add –es.

10. To form the plural of most words that end in –o, such as *potato*
    a. add –ies.
    b. add –en.
    c. add –es.
    d. add –s.

11. To form the plural of most words that end in –f or –fe, such as *knife*,
    a. add –s.
    b. change the –f to a –v and add –es.
    c. add –es.
    d. eliminate the –f and add –ies.

12. When adding a suffix to a word ending in a consonant-vowel-consonant pattern, such as *hop+ ed*,
    a. add an –e before the suffix.
    b. add a hyphen between the word and the suffix.
    c. do not double the final consonant.
    d. double the final consonant.

13. When adding a suffix to a word ending in a vowel and two consonants, two vowels and a consonant, such as *ash* or *book*, such as *book + ed*,
    a. do not double the final consonant.
    b. double the final consonant.
    c. add an –e before the suffix.
    d. add a hyphen between the word and the suffix.

14. When adding a suffix to a word that ends in a nonstressed syllable, such as *happen + ing,*

        a. double the last letter of the word.

        b. add an *–e* before the suffix.

        c. do not double the last letter of the word.

        d. add a hyphen between the word and the suffix.

15. When you add a suffix to most words ending in a consonant before the final *–y,* such as *sleep + ness,*

        a. change the *–y* to an *–i* before adding the suffix.

        b. add an *–e* before the suffix.

        c. add a hyphen between the word and the suffix.

        d. keep the *–y* and add the suffix.

Set 2: Testing Applications

1. Which word in the sentence below is spelled incorrectly?
    Your absence on Wednesday was defiantly a surprise.
    a. absence
    b. Wednesday
    c. defiantly
    d. surprise

2. Which word in the sentence below is spelled incorrectly?
    Tomorrow we must mail our clientele in our foriegn offices.
    a. Tomorrow
    b. clientele
    c. foriegn
    d. offices

3. Which word in the sentence below is spelled incorrectly?
    All atheletes must receive medical clearance before playing.
    a. atheletes
    b. receive
    c. medical
    d. clearance

4. Which word in the sentence below is spelled incorrectly?
    Accommodations for women will be in seperate dormitories.
    a. accommodations
    b. women
    c. seperate
    d. dormitories

5. Identify the incorrectly spelled word below.
    a. leaves
    b. knifes
    c. wolves
    d. calves

6. Identify the incorrectly spelled word below.
    a. necessary
    b. immediately
    c. parallel
    d. convience

7. Identify the incorrectly spelled word below.
      a. beautifull
      b. helpful
      c. careful
      d. wonderful

8. Identify the incorrectly spelled word below.
      a. license
      b. physical
      c. occurr
      d. probably

9. Identify the incorrectly spelled word below.
      a. truely
      b. beginning
      c. thorough
      d. occasion

10. Identify the incorrectly spelled word below.
      a. until
      b. immediately
      c. precious
      d. responsable

11. Identify the incorrectly spelled word below.
      a. grammar
      b. exercise
      c. embarrassing
      d. dilemma

12. Identify the incorrectly spelled word below.
      a. already
      b. recommend
      c. preformance
      d. sincerely

13. Identify the incorrectly spelled word below.
      a. adress
      b. especially
      c. definitely
      d. loneliness

14. Identify the incorrectly spelled word below.
    a. writing
    b. successful
    c. suprise
    d. possess

15. Identify the incorrectly spelled word below.
    a. tomatoes
    b. schedule
    c. mischievous
    d. vaccum

The Writer's World: Sentences and Paragraphs, 3rd Edition
CHAPTER 25: COMMONLY CONFUSED WORDS
Summary

Chapter 25: Commonly Confused Words covers words that students commonly misuse. The chapter begins with a Grammar Snapshot that underlines commonly confused words.

Commonly confused words are explained as those that sound the same but are spelled differently and have different meanings. The chapter is divided into several sections of commonly confused words, divided alphabetically. The first section covers words from *accept* through *compliment*. In Practice 1, students choose the correct words in three passages.

The next section covers the words *conscience* through *no*, and Practice 2 asks students to identify the correct words in three passages. Next addressed are the words *lose* through *principle*, and Practice 3 asks students to edit three passages for errors. The next section covers the words *quiet* through *they're*. Practice 4 asks students to choose the correct word in parentheses in three passages. The final section covers the words *through* through *your*. In Practice 5, students choose the correct word in parentheses in six short passages.

In the Final Review, students edit four passages for errors in word choice. In The Writer's Room, students write about one of two listed topics and proofread their work for spelling or word choice errors. The commonly confused words checklist reminds students to check their work for commonly confused words. In The Writer's Circle, students are instructed to work with a partner to come up with as many homonyms as they can within two minutes. The chapter ends with a referral to MyWritingLab for further review.

The Writer's World: Sentences and Paragraphs, 3rd Edition
CHAPTER 25: COMMONLY CONFUSED WORDS
Exercises

Set 1: Testing Concepts

1. The word *aloud* means
        a. permitted.
        b. in an aggressive or noisy manner.
        c. spoken audibly, out loud.
        d. with confidence.

2. The word *compliment* means
        a. to say something nice about someone or something.
        b. to go with.
        c. to finish.
        d. to add to or complete.

3. The word *except* means
        a. to exclude.
        b. to disregard.
        c. to receive.
        d. to receive or admit.

4. The word *dye* means
        a. to stop living or functioning.
        b. to fade away.
        c. one of a small cube marked with dots.
        d. to color, especially with a coloring compound.

5. The word *fine* means
        a. to locate, especially after a search.
        b. of good quality or a penalty.
        c. to discover.
        d. to realize.

6. The word *it's* is
        a. a possessive form of the pronoun *it*.
        b. is a contraction for *it is*.
        c. is a contraction for *it has*.
        d. both b and c.

7. The word *knew*
    a. means recent or unused.
    b. means packaged or unopened.
    c. means to have knowledge of.
    d. means original or fresh.

8. The word *conscious* means
    a. to be awake or aware.
    b. a personal sense of right or wrong.
    c. a feeling of guilt or innocence.
    d. related to science.

9. The word *every day*
    a. is an adjective meaning common.
    b. is an adverb meaning during a single day or each day.
    c. is an adjective meaning ordinary.
    d. is an adverb meaning not unique.

10. The word *its*
    a. is a contraction for *it is*.
    b. is a contraction for *it has*.
    c. is a possessive case of the pronoun *it*.
    d. both a and b

11. The word *lose* means
    a. to misplace or forfeit something.
    b. not fixed or stationery.
    c. too big or baggy.
    d. not tight.

12. The word *passed* means
    a. a previous time.
    b. a period of time that has already happened.
    c. the past tense of *to pass*, to go beyond or surpass.
    d. both a and b

13. The word *personnel* means
    a. private.
    b. employees or staff.
    c. intimate.
    d. classified.

14. The word *principal* means
   a. a rule or standard.
   b. chief or main.
   c. the director of a school.
   d. both b and c

15. The word *principle* means
   a. chief or main.
   b. the director of a school.
   c. a rule or standard.
   d. both a and b

Set 2: Testing Applications

1. Choose the correctly spelled words for the blanks in the sentence below.
   You can _____ great bargains _____ at this store.
   a. find, every day
   b. fine, every day
   c. find, everyday
   d. fine, everyday

2. Choose the correctly spelled words for the blanks in the sentence below.
   Coach Ralph _____ us how to _____ with honor.
   a. thought, loose
   b. taught, lose
   c. thought, lose
   d. taught, loose

3. Choose the correctly spelled words for the blanks in the sentence below.
   For young, active children, _____ very _____ .

   a. their, quite
   b. they're, quit
   c. their, quiet
   d. they're, quiet

4. Choose the correctly spelled words for the blanks in the sentence below.
   Byron's unexpected _____ had a positive _____ on my mood.
   a. complement, affect
   b. compliment, affect
   c. complement, effect
   d. compliment, effect

5. Choose the correctly spelled words for the blanks in the sentence below.
   _____ _____ for dessert; the pie is already gone.
   a. Your, too
   b. You're, too
   c. Your, to
   d. You're, to

6. Choose the correctly spelled words for the blanks in the sentence below.
   We must _____ the fact that poor customer service is the _____ reason for low sales.
   a. accept, principle
   b. except, principal
   c. accept, principal
   d. except, principle

7. Choose the correctly spelled words for the blanks in the sentence below.
   I drove _____ my exit because I wasn't sure _____ to turn.
   a. past, where
   b. passed, where
   c. past, were
   d. passed, were

8. Choose the correctly spelled words for the blanks in the sentence below.
   Do you know _____ meeting _____ flight?
   a. whose, you're
   b. who's, you're
   c. who's, your
   d. whose, your

9. Choose the correctly spelled words for the blanks in the sentence below.
   _____ hotter today _____ yesterday.
   a. It's, than
   b. It's, then
   c. Its, than
   d. Its, then

10. Choose the correctly spelled words for the blanks in the sentence below.
    Steve _____ that dropping algebra would _____ his scholarship.
    a. new, effect
    b. new, affect
    c. knew, effect
    d. knew, affect

11. Choose the correctly spelled words for the blanks in the sentence below.
    Because she is honest, Clair's clear _____ gives her _____ of mind.
    a. conscious, peace
    b. conscience, peace
    c. conscious, piece
    d. conscience, piece

12. Choose the correctly spelled words for the blanks in the sentence below.
    _____ too bad that our team lost _____ homecoming game.
    a. Its, its
    b. It's, it's
    c. It's, its
    d. Its, it's

13. Choose the correctly spelled words for the blanks in the sentence below.

   The band members are _____ adept with _____ dance steps.
   a. quiet, there
   b. quiet, their
   c. quite, their
   d. quite, there

14. Choose the correctly spelled words for the blanks in the sentence below.

   Do you know _____ _____ going for dinner?
   a. where, we're
   b. were, we're
   c. where, were
   d. we're, were

15. Choose the correctly spelled words for the blanks in the sentence below.

   _____ beginning to look as if _____ right.
   a. Its, your
   b. It's, your
   c. Its, you're
   d. It's, you're

The Writer's World: Sentences and Paragraphs, 3rd Edition
CHAPTER 26: COMMAS
Summary

Chapter 26: Commas covers all comma rules. The chapter begins with a Grammar Snapshot, a passage demonstrating the use of various commas.

The first comma rule introduced is commas in a series. Examples are provided of a series of nouns, verbs, and phrases. In the hint box, students are advised not to place a comma after the last item in the series. In Practice 1, students add missing commas in ten sentences.

Commas after introductory words are explained, and examples of introductory interjections, adverbs, transitional expressions, and introductory phrases are demonstrated in examples. In Practice 2, students identify introductory words and phrases in two passages and add commas.

Commas around interrupting words and phrases are next discussed. Examples are provided, and a hint box explains how to use commas with appositives. In Practice 3, students identify interrupting phrases in eight sentences and add necessary commas. Practice 4 asks students to add missing commas in two passages.

The next rule is commas in compound sentences. Examples are provided, and a hint box reminds students not to use commas before conjunctions that do not separate complete sentences. In Practice 5, students add missing commas in four sentences. In Practice 6, review, students add missing commas to a personal letter.

Commas in complex sentences are introduced; the rule includes commas after introductory dependent clauses. In Practice 7, students edit ten sentences for comma errors. Commas with nonrestrictive clauses are introduced, and examples are provided. A hint box specifies the rules for using commas with *which, that,* and *who.* In Practice 8, students identify relative clauses and add commas where necessary in ten sentences.

Commas in business letters are next introduced. Examples are provided for commas in addresses and dates, and a hint box explains how to use commas with numbers in dates. Commas after salutations and complimentary closings are also explained, and examples are provided. In Practice 9, students add missing commas to a business letter.

In the Final Review, students edit three passages for comma errors. In The Writer's Room, students write about one of two listed topics, making sure to apply comma rules correctly. A comma checklist lists key commas rules, with examples. The chapter ends with a referral to MyWritingLab for supplemental review.

Set 1: Testing Concepts

1. A comma is a punctuation mark that
    a. helps keep distinct ideas separate.
    b. establishes possession and contractions.
    c. ends a sentence.
    d. all of the above

2. Use a comma to separate items in a series
    a. of one or more items. Use a comma after the final item.
    b. of one or more items. Do not use a comma after the final item.
    c. of two or more items. Use a comma before the final *and* or *or*.
    d. of three or more items. Use a comma before the final *and* or *or*.

3. When words or phrases interrupt a sentence,
    a. place a comma before but not after the interrupting words.
    b. place a comma after but not before interrupting words.
    c. do not use commas before or after interrupting words.
    d. place a comma before and after interrupting words.

4. Place a comma
    a. after introductory words or phrases.
    b. after all coordinating conjunctions.
    c. before all dependent clauses.
    d. before introductory words.

5. In the sentence below, thewords that come after the noun and add further informationare called
    Tony, our group leader, does not always make good decisions.
    a. a conjunction.
    b. an appositive.
    c. a dependent clause.
    d. a series.

6. When you join two sentences with a coordinating conjunction (*and, but, for, or, nor, so, yet*),
    a. use a comma after the coordinating conjunction.
    b. use a comma before and after the coordinating conjunction.
    c. do not use commas.
    d. use a comma before the coordinating conjunction.

7. Appositives
   a. are set off with commas.
   b. can appear at the beginning, middle, or end of a sentence.
   c. both a and b
   d. can appear only in the middle of a sentence.

8. If a sentence begins with a dependent clause (beginning with a subordinator such as *because, although, if,* or *when*),
   a. the comma after the dependent clause is optional.
   b. use a comma after the subordinating word and after the clause.
   c. do not use a comma after the dependent clause.
   d. use a comma after the dependent clause.

9. If a dependent clause beginning with a subordinating conjunction such as *because, although, if,* or *when* comes in the middle of a sentence,
   a. the comma before the dependent clause is optional.
   b. use a comma before and after the subordinating word.
   c. do not use a comma before the dependent clause.
   d. use a comma before the dependent clause.

10. In interrupting relative clauses beginning with *who, which,* or *that*, if the relative clause contains nonessential information about the subject,
   a. use commas before and after the clause.
   b. do not use commas before or after the clause.
   c. commas are optional.
   d. use a comma before but not after the clause.

11. In interrupting relative clauses beginning with *who, which,* or *that*, if the relative clause contains essential information about the subject,
   a. use commas before and after the clause.
   b. do not use commas before or after the clause.
   c. commas are optional.
   d. use a comma before but not after the clause.

12. If the sentence includes an interrupting relative clause that begins with *that,*
   a. use commas before and after the clause.
   b. use a comma before the clause but not after.
   c. use a comma after the clause but not before.
   d. do not use commas to set it off.

13. If the sentence includes an interrupting relative clause that begins with *which,*
   a. use commas before and after the clause.
   b. use a comma before the clause but not after.
   c. use a comma after the clause but not before.
   d. do not use commas to set it off.

14. In business letters,
      a. use a comma after the complimentary closing.
      b. use a comma after the salutation.
      c. at the top of the letter, use a comma between the date and the year.
      d. all of the above

15. In the address at the top of a business letter,
      a. put a comma before the zip code.
      b. put a comma between the street and the apartment number.
      c. do not put a comma between the city and state or country.
      d. all of the above

Set 2: Testing Applications

1. Choose the sentence that is punctuated correctly.
   a. Shane doesn't care for Aunt Beth's pumpkin pie, but he ate it anyway.
   b. Shane doesn't care for Aunt Beth's pumpkin pie but, he ate it anyway.
   c. Shane doesn't care for Aunt Beth's pumpkin pie, but, he ate it anyway.
   d. Shane doesn't care for Aunt Beth's pumpkin pie, but he ate it anyway.

2. Choose the sentence that is punctuated correctly.
   a. After the floors are swept they must be mopped and waxed.
   b. After the floors are swept, they must be mopped and waxed.
   c. After, the floors are swept they must be mopped and waxed.
   d. After the floors are swept; they must be mopped and waxed.

3. Choose the sentence that is punctuated correctly.
   a. Breakfast consisted of bagels fresh fruit, and yogurt.
   b. Breakfast consisted of bagels fresh fruit and yogurt.
   c. Breakfast consisted of bagels, fresh fruit, and yogurt.
   d. Breakfast consisted of bagels, fresh fruit and, yogurt.

4. Choose the sentence that is punctuated correctly.
   a. The radio comes with an AC charger, but not with batteries.
   b. The radio comes with an AC charger but, not with batteries.
   c. The radio comes with an AC charger but not with batteries.
   d. The radio comes with an AC charger but not, with batteries.

5. Choose the sentence that is punctuated correctly.
   a. If you are ever in Denver, please come by to visit us.
   b. If you are ever in Denver please come by to visit us.
   c. If you are ever, in Denver please come by to visit us.
   d. If you are ever in Denver, please come by, to visit us.

6. Choose the sentence that is punctuated correctly.
   a. Dennis owns a travel trailer, that has a gas fireplace.
   b. Dennis owns a travel trailer that, has a gas fireplace.
   c. Dennis, owns a travel trailer, that has a gas fireplace.
   d. Dennis owns a travel trailer that has a gas fireplace.

7. Choose the sentence that is punctuated correctly.
   a. Mike lives in Hood River which is on the bank of the Columbia River.
   b. Mike lives in Hood River, which is on the bank of the Columbia River.
   c. Mike lives in Hood River; which is on the bank of the Columbia River.
   d. Mike lives in Hood River which, is on the bank of the Columbia River.

8. Choose the sentence that is punctuated correctly.
   a. Our bicycle club needs someone who can repair bicycles.
   b. Our bicycle club needs someone, who can repair bicycles.
   c. Our bicycle club needs someone who, can repair bicycles.
   d. Our bicycle club, needs someone who can repair bicycles.

9. Choose the sentence that is punctuated correctly.
   a. Actress Gwyneth Paltrow, for example also sings.
   b. Actress Gwyneth Paltrow, for example, also sings.
   c. Actress Gwyneth Paltrow for example also sings.
   d. Actress Gwyneth Paltrow for example, also sings.

10. Choose the sentence that is punctuated correctly.
    a. The SGA president, Jill Wilson will speak at today's faculty meeting.
    b. The SGA president Jill Wilson, will speak at today's faculty meeting.
    c. The SGA president, Jill Wilson, will speak at today's faculty meeting.
    d. The SGA president Jill Wilson will speak at today's faculty meeting.

11. Choose the sentence that is punctuated correctly.
    a. Ryan and Ann have a swimming pool yet rarely use it.
    b. Ryan and Ann have a swimming pool, yet rarely use it.
    c. Ryan and Ann have a swimming pool yet, rarely use it.
    d. Ryan and Ann have a swimming pool, yet, rarely use it.

12. Choose the sentence that is punctuated correctly.
    a. This year's conference will be held in Miami, Florida in July.
    b. This year's conference will be held in Miami Florida in July.
    c. This year's conference will be held in Miami Florida, in July.
    d. This year's conference will be held in Miami, Florida, in July.

13. Choose the sentence that is punctuated correctly.
    a. Matt is one of the pilots, who flew at the air show.
    b. Matt is one of the pilots who, flew at the air show.
    c. Matt is one of the pilots who flew at the air show.
    d. Matt is one, of the pilots, who flew at the air show.

14. Choose the sentence that is punctuated correctly.
    a. Send your application to 1400 Marcos Street, Boise, Idaho 96000.
    b. Send your application to 1400 Marcos Street, Boise, Idaho, 96000.
    c. Send your application to 1400 Marcos Street Boise, Idaho 96000.
    d. Send your application to 1400 Marcos Street Boise Idaho 96000.

15. Choose the sentence that is punctuated correctly.
    a. School closed early today, because there was a power failure.
    b. School closed early today because there was a power failure.
    c. School closed early today; because, there was a power failure.
    d. School closed early today because, there was a power failure.

196
Copyright © 2011, 2009, 2006 Pearson Education, Inc.

The Writer's World: Sentences and Paragraphs, 3rd Edition
CHAPTER 27: THE APOSTROPHE

Summary

Chapter 27: The Apostrophe covers apostrophe use in contractions, in ownership, and in expressions of time. The chapter opens with a Grammar Snapshot of a passage demonstrating various apostrophe use.

Apostrophes with contractions are explained, and examples are provided. A hint box advises students to avoid using contractions in formal academic papers. A chart showing common contractions is provided, and in Practice 1, students create contractions for words in six sentences. Contractions formed by subjects plus verbs are explained, with a list of common contractions. A hint box shows how to contract a proper noun with *be* or *have*. In Practice 2, students add missing apostrophes in three passages. Another hint box points out contractions with two meanings. In Practice 3, students translate contractions in five sentences into complete words.

Using apostrophes to show ownership is discussed next. Each rule is explained, and several examples are provided. In Practice 4, students create possessive forms for ten items. In Practice 5, students edit two passages for errors in possessive apostrophes.

The final section of this chapter covers apostrophes in expressions of time. Examples are provided, and a hint box cautions students to avoid using apostrophes on verbs and to avoid confusing contractions with possessive pronouns. In Practice 6, students edit ten sentences for errors in apostrophes.

In the Final Review, students edit passages for errors in all types of apostrophes. In The Writer's Room, students write about one of two listed topics, ensuring that they have used apostrophes correctly. The apostrophe checklist provides a brief list of apostrophe rules with examples. The chapter ends with a referral to MyWritingLab for further review.

The Writer's World: Sentences and Paragraphs, 3ʳᵈ Edition
CHAPTER 27: THE APOSTROPHE
Exercises

Set 1: Testing Concepts

1. An apostrophe is a punctuation mark that shows
    a. that two words have been contracted into one.
    b. ownership.
    c. plurals of nouns.
    d. both a and b

2. When an apostrophe is used in a contraction, the apostrophe generally indicates
    a. a plural noun or pronoun.
    b. a missing phrase.
    c. the location of the omitted letter or letters.
    d. possession.

3. You should not use contractions in
    a. formal academic papers.
    b. casual writing.
    c. email messages.
    d. personal letters.

4. The contraction *we're* means
    a. we have been
    b. we are
    c. we are being
    d. all of the above.

5. _____ use an apostrophe to show ownership.
    a. Pronouns and adjectives
    b. Verbs and adverbs
    c. Verbs
    d. Nouns and indefinite pronouns

6. To show possession of singular nouns,
    a. add an *–s'* to the end of the singular noun.
    b. add *–s's* to the end of the singular noun.
    c. add *– 's* to the end of the singular noun.
    d. add just an *–s* to the end of a singular noun.

7. To show possession of plural nouns that end in –s,
   a. add an –s, an apostrophe, and another –s to the end of a plural noun.
   b. the apostrophe is optional.
   c. add an –s and an apostrophe to the end of a plural noun.
   d. add just an apostrophe after the final –s.

8. To show possession of irregular plural nouns (those that change spelling rather than take –s or –es),
   a. add an –s and an apostrophe to the final letter.
   b. add an apostrophe and an –s to the final letter.
   c. add just an apostrophe after the final letter.
   d. add just an –s after the final letter.

9. When two people have joint ownership of something,
   a. add the apostrophe to the second name only.
   b. omit the apostrophes.
   c. add the apostrophe to both names.
   d. add the apostrophe to the first name only.

10. When two people have separate ownership,
   a. add the apostrophe to the second name only.
   b. omit the apostrophes.
   c. add the apostrophe to both names.
   d. add the apostrophe to the first name only.

11. If you wanted to express that someone had paid ten dollars for gas, you could express the amount as
   a. ten dollar's worth of gas
   b. ten dollars worth of gas
   c. ten dollars' worth of gas'
   d. ten dollars' worth of gas.

12. Which of the following possessive pronouns requires an apostrophe?
   a. hers
   b. theirs
   c. yours
   d. none of the above

13. If you wanted to write out a year using just the last two numerals, you could write the number as
   a. the class of 87'.
   b. the class of '87.
   c. the class of '87'.
   d. the class of 87.

14. Which of the following expressions shows possession?
    a. Jennifer's book
    b. Let's go!
    c. It's time for dinner.
    d. Who's in charge here?

15. Which of the following expressions shows a contraction?
    a. the eagle's nest
    b. It doesn't work.
    c. someone else's cell phone
    d. all of the above

Set 2: Testing Applications

1. Which sentence uses contractions correctly?
    a. Who's doing your landscaping work?
    b. Whose doing your landscaping work?
    c. Who's doing you're landscaping work?
    d. Who's doing you're landscaping work?

2. Which sentence uses contractions correctly?
    a. Let's tell the utility service that it's policies are unfair.
    b. Lets tell the utility service that its policies are unfair.
    c. Let's tell the utility service that its policies are unfair.
    d. Lets tell the utility service that it's policies are unfair.

3. Which sentence uses contractions correctly?
    a. Did you know that were babysitting their dog this weekend?
    b. Did you know that we're babysitting they're dog this weekend?
    c. Did you know that were babysitting they're dog this weekend?
    d. Did you know that we're babysitting their dog this weekend?

4. Which sentence uses apostrophes correctly?
    a. Several students have already signed up for Professor Blakes course.
    b. Several students have already signed up for Professor Blake's course.
    c. Several students' have already signed up for Professor Blakes course.
    d. Several students' have already signed up for Professor Blake's course.

5. Which sentence uses apostrophes correctly?
    a. All of the auditors couldn't have missed that serious error.
    b. All of the auditor's couldn't have missed that serious error.
    c. All of the auditors could'nt have missed that serious error.
    d. All of the auditor's could'nt have missed that serious error.

6. Which sentence uses apostrophes correctly?
    a. Do you realize that it's a full day's drive to Denver?
    b. Do you realize that it's a full days drive to Denver?
    c. Do you realize that its a full day's drive to Denver?
    d. Do you realize that its a full days' drive to Denver?

7. Which sentence uses apostrophes correctly?
    a. We're ready to look at someone elses bid for this job.
    b. Were ready to look at someone elses bid for this job.
    c. We're ready to look at someone else's bid for this job.
    d. Were ready to look at someone else's bid for this job.

8. Which sentence uses apostrophes correctly?
   a. Who's cell phone is ringing? Is it hers'?
   b. Whose cell phone is ringing? Is it hers'?
   c. Who's cell phone is ringing? Is it hers?
   d. Whose cell phone is ringing? Is it hers?

9. Which sentence uses apostrophes correctly?
   a. My grandparents' home is high in the Colorado Rockies.
   b. My grandparent's home is high in the Colorado Rockies.
   c. My grandparents' home is high in the Colorado Rockies'.
   d. My grandparent's home is high in the Colorado Rockies'.

10. Which sentence uses apostrophes correctly?
    a. Evan bought ten dollars worth of junk food and a dollars worth of gas.
    b. Evan bought ten dollar's worth of junk food and a dollar's worth of gas.
    c. Evan bought ten dollars' worth of junk food and a dollar's worth of gas.
    d. Evan bought ten dollars' worth of junk food and a dollars worth of gas.

11. Which sentence uses apostrophes correctly?
    a. I believe those book's are theirs.
    b. I believe those books are theirs'.
    c. I believe those books are theirs.
    d. I believe those books' are theirs'.

12. Which sentence uses apostrophes correctly?
    a. A few employees' mistakes have cost the company a week's work.
    b. A few employees mistakes have cost the company a week's work.
    c. A few employee's mistakes have cost the company a weeks work.
    d. A few employees' mistakes have cost the company a weeks' work.

13. Which sentence uses apostrophes correctly?
    a. Everyones' pay check should be in tomorrow's mail.
    b. Everyone's pay check should be in tomorrows mail.
    c. Everyones pay check should be in tomorrow's mail.
    d. Everyone's pay check should be in tomorrow's mail.

14. Which sentence uses apostrophes correctly?
    a. They're planning on some downsizing in your department.
    b. There planning on some downsizing in you're department.
    c. They're planning on some downsizing in you're department.
    d. There planning on some downsizing in your department.

15. Which sentence uses apostrophes correctly?
    a. My families church will hold it's holiday bazaar in November.
    b. My family's church will hold its holiday bazaar in November.
    c. My familys church will hold its holiday bazaar in November.
    d. My family's church will hold it's holiday bazaar in November.

Chapter 28: Quotation Marks and Capitalization covers direct and indirect quotations, quotation marks, capitalization, and titles. The chapter opens with a Grammar Snapshot that demonstrates quotation marks and capitalization.

The difference between direct and indirect quotations is explained, and examples are provided. Quotation marks are defined and illustrated by examples. Using quotation marks with introductory phrases is explained, and in Practice 1, students add quotation marks in five sentences. Using quotation marks with interrupting phrases is also explained, and Practice 2 asks students to add quotation marks in five sentences. Using quotation marks with an end phrase is explained, followed by examples. In Practice 3, students add quotation marks, capital letters, and other punctuation in five sentences. The last rule in this section addresses using quotation marks with an introductory sentence. Examples are provided, and in Practice 4, students add quotation marks in five sentences. In Practice 5, students add quotation marks, capital letters, and other punctuation in three passages.

Capitalization is then introduced. All rules are explained and followed by examples. A hint box provides information on capitalizing computer terms. In Practice 6, students add capital letters as needed in ten sentences.

Punctuating titles is addressed, with a chart illustrating quotation marks versus underlining. Capitalizing titles is also discussed, and examples are presented. In Practice 7, students add capital letters, quotation marks, or underlining in a paragraph.

In the Final Review, students edit two passages for quotation marks and capitalization. In The Writer's Room, students write about one of two topics listed and then identify words that they have capitalized or placed in quotation marks. The checklist provides a brief review of key rules. In The Writer's Circle, students are instructed to work with a partner. One dictates dialogue from an essay in this book while the other writes down the passage to practice using quotation marks and capitalization correctly. At chapter's end, students are directed to MyWritingLab for further review.

Set 1: Testing Concepts

1. An indirect quotation
    a. summarizes someone's words.
    b. does not use quotation marks.
    c. reproduces the exact words of a speaker or writer.
    d. both a and b.

2. A direct quotation
    a. identifies words that are emphasized or being used in a special sense.
    c. reproduces the exact words of a speaker or writer.
    d. summarizes someone's words.
    d. all of the above

3. Indirect quotations often begin with the word
    a. *that.*
    b. *when.*
    c. *who.*
    d. *which.*

4. Quotation marks are used to
    a. indicate clichés.
    b. indicate a speaker's summarized words.
    c. set off the exact words of a speaker of writer.
    d. all of the above

5. If a quoted passage is a complete sentence,
    a. capitalize the first word of the quotation.
    b. place quotation marks around the complete quotation.
    c. place the end punctuation inside the closing quotation marks.
    d. all of the above

6. When the quotation is introduced by an introductory phrase such as *he said,*
    a. no punctuation is used.
    b. punctuation is optional.
    c. place a semicolon after the introductory phrase.
    d. place a comma after the introductory phrase.

7. If you introduce a quotation with a complete sentence,
  a. no punctuation is used.
  b. place a comma after the introductory sentence.
  c. place a semicolon after the introductory sentence.
  c. either b or c

8. When you place a phrase at the end of a quotation, such as *he said* or *she said,*
  a. end the quotation with a semicolon.
  b. no punctuation is used.
  c. end the quotation with a comma instead of a period.
  d. end the quotation with a period.

9. Always capitalize
  a. the first word of every sentence.
  b. the days of the week.
  c. the pronoun *I.*
  d. all of the above.

10. Which of the following should NOT be capitalized?
  a. the seasons of the year
  b. the pronoun *I*
  c. the months of the year
  d. the names of holidays

11. Which of the following should NOT be capitalized?
  a. the names of specific buildings, streets, parks, cities, and bodies of water
  b. specific languages, nationalities, tribes, races, and religions
  c. titles of specific institutions, departments, companies, and schools
  d. names of general references to institutions, departments, companies, and schools

12. Which of the following should NOT be capitalized?
  a. the names of specific persons
  b. names of professions
  c. the titles of specific courses with numbers
  d. major words in titles of literary works

13. Which of the following should NOT be capitalized?
  a. historical eras
  b. names of religions
  c. historical events such as named wars
  d. general references to academic subjects

14. Which of the following should NOT be capitalized?
   a. the titles of specific college courses with numbers
   b. breeds of animals unless based on a proper noun
   c. the names of Internet browsers
   d. all of the above

15. Which of the following should NOT be capitalized?
   a. names of ships
   b. professional titles when they come right before the person's name
   c. short prepositions in titles of literary works
   d. titles of paintings

Set 2: Testing Applications

1. Which sentence is punctuated correctly?
   a. "The coffee is ready", said Cliff.
   b. "The coffee is ready," said Cliff.
   c. "The coffee is ready." said Cliff.
   d. "The coffee is ready, said Cliff."

2. Which sentence is punctuated correctly?
   a. Crystal said that "she signed up for a yoga class."
   b. Crystal said "that she signed up for a yoga class."
   c. Crystal said that, "She signed up for a yoga class."
   d. Crystal said that she signed up for a yoga class.

3. Which sentence is punctuated correctly?
   a. "My cat," said Dan. "Has learned how to shake hands."
   b. "My cat", said Dan, "has learned how to shake hands".
   c. "My cat," said Dan, "has learned how to shake hands."
   d. "My cat, said Dan, has learned how to shake hands."

4. Which sentence is punctuated correctly?
   a. Eric asked us, "Have you seen my briefcase?"
   b. Eric asked us "if we had seen his briefcase."
   c. Eric asked us. "Have you seen my briefcase?"
   d. Eric asked us, "if we had seen his briefcase?"

5. Which sentence uses capitalization correctly?
   a. My only days off this spring will be spring break.
   b. My only days off this Spring will be Spring Break.
   c. My only days off this spring will be Spring Break.
   d. My only days off this Spring will be spring break.

6. Which sentence is punctuated correctly?
   a. "Have you seen Julia Roberts' latest movie," Maya asked.
   b. "Have you seen Julia Roberts' latest movie?" Maya asked.
   c. "Have you seen Julia Roberts' latest movie, Maya asked?"
   d. "Have you seen Julia Roberts' latest movie"? Maya asked.

7. Which sentence uses capitalization correctly?
   a. Brad received a degree in Psychology from Colorado State University.
   b. Brad received a degree in psychology from Colorado state university.
   c. Brad received a degree in Psychology from Colorado state university.
   d. Brad received a degree in psychology from Colorado State University.

8. Which sentence uses capitalization correctly?
    a. I need one course in english and two courses in history to finish my degree.
    b. I need one course in english and two courses in History to finish my degree.
    c. I need one course in English and two courses in History to finish my degree.
    d. I need one course in English and two courses in history to finish my degree.

9. Which sentence uses capitalization correctly?
    a. Michelle is a baptist, and her sister is a lutheran.
    b. Michelle is a Baptist, and her sister is a lutheran.
    c. Michelle is a Baptist, and her sister is a Lutheran.
    d. Michelle is a baptist, and her sister is a Lutheran.

10. Which sentence uses capitalization correctly?
    a. In the fall, our community hosts a Thanksgiving festival.
    b. In the Fall, our community hosts a Thanksgiving festival.
    c. In the Fall, our community hosts a thanksgiving festival.
    d. In the fall, our community hosts a thanksgiving festival.

11. Which sentence uses capitalization correctly?
    a. I can't believe that my Mother has signed up for Philosophy 2000.
    b. I can't believe that my mother has signed up for philosophy 2000.
    c. I can't believe that my mother has signed up for Philosophy 2000.
    d. I can't believe that my Mother has signed up for philosophy 2000.

12. Which sentence uses capitalization correctly?
    a. Malcolm is an FBI Agent who works near times square in New York.
    b. Malcolm is an FBI agent who works near Times Square in New York.
    c. Malcolm is an FBI Agent who works near Times Square in New York.
    d. Malcolm is an FBI agent who works near times square in New York.

13. Which sentence uses capitalization correctly?
    a. I have heard that Doctor Norman is an excellent Physician.
    b. I have heard that Doctor Norman is an excellent physician.
    c. I have heard that doctor norman is an excellent physician.
    d. I have heard that doctor Norman is an excellent Physician.

14. Which sentence uses capitalization correctly?
   a. On Independence Day, we plan to visit our Uncle's lake house in Georgia.
   b. On independence day, we plan to visit our uncle's lake house in Georgia.
   c. On Independence Day, we plan to visit our uncle's lake house in Georgia.
   d. On independence day, we plan to visit our Uncle's lake house in Georgia.

15. Which sentence uses capitalization correctly?
   a. My mother loves the movie "Gone with the Wind."
   b. My Mother loves the movie "Gone with the Wind."
   c. My mother loves the movie "Gone With The Wind."
   d. My Mother loves the movie "Gone With The Wind."

The Writer's World: Sentences and Paragraphs, 3rd Edition
CHAPTER 29: EDITING PRACTICE
Summary

Chapter 29: Editing Practice explains the importance of editing their writing for grammar, punctuation, sentence structure, and capitalization.

Practice 1 asks students to correct underlined errors in a paragraph and refers them to the editing symbols on the inside front cover of their book. In Practice 2, students edit a passage that contains no editing symbols. In Practice 3, students proofread and correct errors in a passage that has no proofreading symbols. In Practice 4, students edit a business memo for errors. In Practices 5 and 6, students correct errors in passages. In Practice 7 students identify and correct errors in a student essay. The chapter ends with a referral to MyWritingLab for further review.

Set 1: Testing Concepts

1. Editing means to
   a. delete sentences and paragraphs that do not support the main point.
   b. add sentences and paragraphs to more fully support the main point.
   c. revise your writing for content and organization.
   d. review your work for errors in grammar, punctuation, sentence structure, and capitalization.

2. The editing symbol *sp* refers to
   a. spelling.
   b. secondary punctuation.
   c. spacing.
   d. special punctuation.

3. The editing symbol *sv* refers to
   a. a point that can be argued.
   b. an inappropriate tone.
   c. a subject-verb agreement error.
   d. a shift in voice.

4. The editing symbol *frag* refers to
   a. a run-on sentence.
   b. a fragment, or incomplete, sentence.
   c. a missing comma.
   d. a dangling modifier.

5. The editing symbol *ro* refers to
   a. a form used only on rare occasions.
   b. a rough transition.
   c. an obsolete rule.
   d. a run-on sentence.

6. The editing symbol *vt* refers to
   a. a verb tense error.
   b. a transitive verb.
   c. "very truly."
   d. very tight writing.

7. The editing symbol *pro* refers to
    a. a pronoun error.
    b. a profound error.
    c. a professional term, or jargon.
    d. information that requires the writer to provide supporting evidence.

8. The editing symbol *p* refers to
    a. a preposition error.
    b. a punctuation error.
    c. a pronoun-antecedent agreement error.
    d. a possible error.

9. The editing symbol *ad* refers to
    a. an advertising term.
    b. an advantageous term.
    c. a requirement for additional information.
    d. an adjective or adverb error.

10. The editing symbol *m* refers to
    a. a misplaced modifier.
    b. a misspelled word.
    c. a mangled sentence.
    d. a misused word.

11. The editing symbol *wc* refers to
    a. a word choice error.
    b. a wrongly used colon.
    c. a word count error.
    d. a wandering comma.

12. The editing symbol *pl* refers to
    a. a plural error.
    b. a misplaced prepositional phrase.
    c. a word placement error.
    d. a pronoun error.

13. The editing symbol *//* refers to
    a. an inappropriate shift.
    b. a run-on sentence.
    c. an error in parallel structure.
    d. missing punctuation.

14. The editing symbol *shift* refers to
    a. a required shift.
    b. an unnecessary shift.
    c. an abrupt shift in the punctuation.
    d. a shift in paragraph.

15. The editing symbol *p* refers to
    a. a possessive error.
    b. a comma error
    c. a punctuation error.
    d. all of the above.

Set 2: Testing applications

1. Which error occurs in the following sentence?
        Nobody elses lasagna is as good as yours.
    a. comma
    b. misplaced modifier
    c. apostrophe
    d. spelling

2. Which error occurs in the following sentence?
        If our team expects to win, they must play much more aggressive.
    a. capitalization
    b. adjective vs. adverb
    c. subject-verb agreement
    d. spelling

3. Which error occurs in the following sentence?
        Next weekend, me and Chelsea are going to her grandparents' condo.
    a. pronoun case
    b. apostrophe
    c. comma
    d. adjective vs. adverb

4. Which error occurs in the following sentence?
        Be careful. I have just sharpened all the knifes.
    a. plural form spelling error
    b. apostrophe
    c. fragment
    d. parallel structure

5. Which error occurs in the following sentence?
        I'm worried about the barn cats it's very cold outside.
    a. an apostrophe error
    b. comma
    c. run on
    d. fragment

6. Which error occurs in the following sentence?
        Our basketball team must play tonight without it's starting forward.
    a. apostrophe
    b. spelling
    c. comma
    d. fragment

7. Which error occurs in the following sentence?

Last week, Lynn showed up at our house and asks for a place to stay.

a. subject-verb agreement
b. tense shift
c. apostrophe
d. comma

8. Which error occurs in the following sentence?

We packed hurriedly, and left for a weekend getaway.

a. spelling
b. comma
c. parallel structure
d. subject-verb agreement

9. Which error occurs in the following sentence?

Riding my bicycle to class, my dog followed me.

a. apostrophe
b. comma
c. parallel structure
d. dangling modifier

10. Which error occurs in the following sentence?

It's been a rough week for Dennis and I.

a. an apostrophe error
b. parallel structure
c. pronoun case
d. adjective vs. adverb

11. Which error occurs in the following sentence?

You're lucky. You could of gotten seriously injured.

a. apostrophe
b. comma
c. word choice
d. fragment

12. Which error occurs in the following sentence?

I have reserved this weekend to organize my closet, vacuum the carpets, and cleaning the junk drawer.

a. spelling
b. misplaced modifier
c. subject-verb agreement
d. parallel structure

13. Which error occurs in the following sentence?

Kyle, who thrilled fans by running for a sixty-yard touchdown last Saturday.

   a. pronoun case
   b. fragment
   c. parallel structure
   d. tense shift

14. Which error occurs in the following sentence?

We see deer in our back yard nearly everyday.

   a. commonly confused word
   b. adjective vs. adverb
   c. comma
   d. spelling

15. Which error occurs in the following sentence?

Three employees cars were damaged by the falling sign.

   a. fragment
   b. run-on
   c. apostrophe
   d. spelling

Chapter 30: Reading Strategies and Selections presents reading selections to help students develop writing skills.

The chapter begins by explaining that reading helps expand vocabulary, helps learn how other writers develop topics, helps to recognize different writing patterns, and helps to find ideas for students' own writing.

Previewing titles and main headlines, first and last sentences, and topic sentences are explained. Instructions are provided for taking notes, highlighting, and annotating. An example of an annotated passage is presented.

There is a short discussion of using context clues, followed by examples. In Practice 1, students are asked to read words in context to determine their meaning. A hint box advises students that some words have many definitions.

Writing about readings is discussed next, with a discussion about how to respond to readings.

Four readings are presented, and students answer vocabulary and comprehension questions, grammar questions, and discussion and writing questions for each. The four readings are "Fish Cheeks," by Amy Tan; "Birth," by Maya Angelou; "The New Addiction," by Josh Freed; and "Fat Chance," by Dorothy Nixon.

In The Writer's Room, Writing Activity 1, students write about a photograph. In Writing Activity 2, students write about a movie.

Four additional readings are provided, and students answer vocabulary and comprehension questions, grammar questions, and discussion and writing questions for each. The readings are "What is your Humor Style?" by Louise Dobson; "A Cultural Minefield," by William Ecenbarger; "The Cult of Emaciation," by Ben Barry; and "Shopping for Religion," by Ellen Goodman.

In "The Writer's Room," Writing Activity 1, students write about a photograph. In Writing Activity 2, students write about filmmaking.

Four additional readings are presented, and students answer vocabulary and comprehension questions, grammar questions, and discussion and writing questions for each. The readings are "What It Feels Like to Walk on the Moon," by Buzz Aldrin; "The Fire Below," by Bill Bryson; "The Zoo Life," by Yann Martel; and "Is it Love or Trick," by Jon Katz.

In The Writer's Room, Writing Activity 1, students write about one of three topics. In Writing Activity 2, students write about a film.

Five additional readings are presented, , and students answer vocabulary and comprehension questions, grammar questions, and discussion and writing questions for each. The readings are "The Allure of Apple," by Juan Rodriguez; "How to Handle Conflict," by P. Gregory Smith; "How to Remember Names," by Roger Seip; "Meet the Zippies," by Thomas L. Friedman; and "The Rewards of Dirty Work," by Linda L. Lindsey and Stephen Beach.

In The Writer's Room, Writing Activity 1, students write about topics related to technology, and in Writing Activity 2, students write about film. The chapter ends with a referral to MyWritingLab for further review.

The Writer's World: Sentences and Paragraphs, 3rd Edition
Quiz Answer Key

CHAPTER 1: EXPLORING

Set 1

1. b	6. c	11. c
2. c	7. c	12. d
3. d	8. a	13. d
4. a	9. d	14. c
5. d	10. b	15. d

Set 2

1. c	6. a	11. a
2. a	7. d	12. d
3. d	8. c	13. a
4. b	9. a	14. b
5. a	10. b	15. c

CHAPTER 2: DEVELOPING

Set 1

1. d	6. c	11. d
2. a	7. c	12. c
3. d	8. a	13. b
4. a	9. d	14. a
5. d	10. b	15. d

Set 2

1. d	6. a	11. a
2. a	7. b	12. c
3. a	8. d	13. b
4. c	9. c	14. d
5. a	10. b	15. a

CHAPTER 3: REVISING AND EDITING

Set 1

1. c	6. a	11. b
2. d	7. c	12. a
3. c	8. c	13. b
4. b	9. d	14. a
5. b	10. a	15. d

Set 2

1. a	6. d	11. c
2. b	7. a	12. b
3. c	8. d	13. d
4. a	9. b	14. a
5. c	10. d	15. c

CHAPTER 4: PARAGRAPH PATTERNS

Set 1

1. d	6. c	11. d
2. b	7. d	12. b
3. a	8. b	13. d
4. b	9. c	14. b
5. a	10. a	15. c

Set 2

1. a	6. c	11. b
2. b	7. b	12. a
3. a	8. c	13. c
4. d	9. c	14. b
5. d	10. d	15. a

CHAPTER 5: WRITING THE ESSAY

Set 1

1. a	6. d	11. d
2. c	7. b	12. c
3. c	8. d	13. a
4. b	9. a	14. a
5. a	10. c	15. b

Set 2

1. d	6. d	11. d
2. b	7. a	12. d
3. d	8. c	13. a
4. b	9. b	14. b
5. b	10. c	15. a

CHAPTER 6: NOUNS, DETERMINERS, AND PREPOSITIONS

Set 1

1. b	6. c	11. d
2. d	7. d	12. a
3. c	8. b	13. a
4. d	9. c	14. c
5. a	10. c	15. b

Set 2

1. c	6. d	11. b
2. d	7. c	12. a
3. a	8. a	13. a
4. a	9. b	14. c
5. b	10. d	15. d

CHAPTER 7: PRONOUNS

Set 1

1. a	6. c	11. a
2. c	7. d	12. c
3. a	8. d	13. a
4. b	9. b	14. b
5. d	10. c	15. a

Set 2

1. a	6. a	11. a
2. c	7. d	12. b
3. d	8. b	13. b
4. c	9. c	14. a
5. b	10. d	15. d

CHAPTER 8: SUBJECTS AND VERBS

Set 1

1. a	6. a	11. c
2. c	7. c	12. b
3. d	8. c	13. d
4. d	9. d	14. c
5. a	10. a	15. a

Set 2

1. b	6. c	11. c
2. d	7. d	12. d
3. b	8. d	13. a
4. a	9. a	14. a
5. a	10. b	15. c

CHAPTER 9: PRESENT AND PAST TENSES

Set 1

1. d	6. c	11. c
2. a	7. c	12. b
3. b	8. d	13. a
4. c	9. a	14. d
5. b	10. d	15. b

Set 2

1. c	6. b	11. a
2. a	7. c	12. a
3. c	8. d	13. b
4. d	9. a	14. b
5. c	10. c	15. b

CHAPTER 10: PAST PARTICIPLES

Set 1

1. d	6. d	11. b
2. b	7. b	12. a
3. a	8. a	13. b
4. b	9. d	14. c
5. d	10. d	15. a

Set 2

1. a	6. b	11. a
2. d	7. c	12. d
3. c	8. b	13. a
4. d	9. d	14. a
5. a	10. b	15. c

CHAPTER 11: PROGRESSIVE TENSES

Set 1

1. b	6. a	11. a
2. d	7. c	12. c
3. a	8. d	13. c
4. c	9. d	14. b
5. b	10. b	15. a

Set 2

1. d	6. c	11. a
2. a	7. c	12. d
3. c	8. a	13. c
4. a	9. d	14. c
5. b	10. b	15. b

CHAPTER 12: OTHER VERB FORMS

Set 1

1. c	6. b	11. c
2. a	7. d	12. d
3. c	8. b	13. c
4. d	9. a	14. a
5. c	10. a	15. b

Set 2

1. d	6. d	11. c
2. a	7. d	12. a
3. c	8. a	13. a
4. b	9. a	14. d
5. b	10. d	15. c

CHAPTER 13: SUBJECT-VERB AGREEMENT

Set 1

1. d	6. d	11. c
2. c	7. b	12. b
3. b	8. c	13. a
4. a	9. d	14. d
5. d	10. a	15. a

Set 2

1. c	6. c	11. d
2. b	7. c	12. a
3. a	8. b	13. d
4. d	9. a	14. c
5. b	10. c	15. b

CHAPTER 14: TENSE CONSISTENCY

Set 1

1. d	6. b	11. c
2. a	7. d	12. a
3. b	8. c	13. d
4. d	9. a	14. c
5. b	10. b	15. b

Set 2

1. b	6. a	11. c
2. a	7. a	12. a
3. d	8. c	13. d
4. b	9. d	14. d
5. c	10. b	15. b

CHAPTER 15: COMPOUND SENTENCES

Set 1

1. c	6. b	11. d
2. a	7. d	12. a
3. d	8. c	13. b
4. b	9. a	14. b
5. a	10. b	15. d

Set 2

1. a	6. a	11. d
2. d	7. b	12. a
3. b	8. c	13. c
4. c	9. b	14. b
5. d	10. a	15. b

CHAPTER 16: COMPLEX SENTENCES

Set 1

1. c	6. a	11. d
2. b	7. c	12. b
3. a	8. d	13. b
4. d	9. a	14. a
5. b	10. b	15. c

Set 2

1. d	6. c	11. d
2. c	7. c	12. a
3. b	8. a	13. c
4. a	9. b	14. a
5. c	10. d	15. b

CHAPTER 17: SENTENCE VARIETY

Set 1

1. a	6. c	11. b
2. d	7. c	12. a
3. c	8. b	13. d
4. b	9. a	14. c
5. a	10. d	15. b

Set 2

1. a	6. a	11. a
2. c	7. c	12. b
3. d	8. c	13. b
4. b	9. b	14. d
5. c	10. d	15. a

CHAPTER 18: FRAGMENTS

Set 1

1. d	6. a	11. b
2. d	7. b	12. c
3. c	8. d	13. c
4. a	9. c	14. a
5. b	10. d	15. d

Set 2

1. c	6. c	11. a
2. b	7. a	12. b
3. b	8. d	13. c
4. d	9. b	14. c
5. a	10. c	15. d

CHAPTER 19: RUN-ONS

Set 1

1. c	6. b	11. c
2. a	7. a	12. a
3. d	8. c	13. c
4. a	9. d	14. a
5. c	10. b	15. d

Set 2

1. c	6. b	11. b
2. d	7. c	12. c
3. b	8. d	13. b
4. a	9. a	14. d
5. c	10. a	15. c

CHAPTER 20: FAULTY PARALLEL STRUCTURE

Set 1

1. b	6. d	11. c
2. d	7. d	12. b
3. d	8. b	13. a
4. c	9. a	14. d
5. a	10. c	15. d

Set 2

1. b	6. c	11. a
2. d	7. a	12. a
3. c	8. d	13. d
4. d	9. c	14. c
5. a	10. b	15. b

CHAPTER 21: ADJECTIVES AND ADVERBS

Set 1
1. a
2. c
3. d
4. b
5. a
6. d
7. c
8. b
9. b
10. d
11. d
12. b
13. a
14. b
15. c

Set 2
1. d
2. c
3. b
4. a
5. d
6. b
7. c
8. a
9. d
10. c
11. d
12. a
13. b
14. d
15. c

CHAPTER 22: MISTAKES WITH MODIFIERS

Set 1
1. c
2. a
3. c
4. a
5. d
6. c
7. d
8. c
9. a
10. b
11. b
12. c
13. d
14. b
15. a

Set 2
1. a
2. c
3. b
4. d
5. c
6. a
7. a
8. d
9. c
10. b
11. a
12. c
13. b
14. d
15. b

CHAPTER 23: EXACT LANGUAGE

Set 1
1. d
2. c
3. a
4. b
5. b
6. d
7. c
8. a
9. b
10. d
11. c
12. a
13. b
14. d
15. c

Set 2

1. d 6. d 11. c
2. c 7. a 12. a
3. a 8. d 13. b
4. b 9. b 14. d
5. c 10. b 15. c

CHAPTER 24: SPELLING

Set 1

1. b 6. b 11. b
2. c 7. c 12. d
3. a 8. a 13. a
4. c 9. d 14. c
5. d 10. c 15. a

Set 2

1. c 6. d 11. b
2. c 7. a 12. c
3. a 8. c 13. a
4. c 9. a 14. c
5. b 10. d 15. d

CHAPTER 25: COMMONLY CONFUSED WORDS

Set 1

1. c 6. d 11. a
2. a 7. b 12. c
3. a 8. a 13. b
4. d 9. d 14. d
5. b 10. d 15. c

Set 2

1. a 6. c 11. b
2. b 7. a 12. c
3. d 8. c 13. c
4. d 9. a 14. a
5. b 10. d 15. c

CHAPTER 26: COMMAS

Set 1

1. a	6. d	11. b
2. c	7. c	12. d
3. d	8. d	13. a
4. a	9. c	14. d
5. b	10. a	15. b

Set 2

1. d	6. d	11. a
2. b	7. b	12. d
3. c	8. a	13. c
4. c	9. b	14. a
5. a	10. c	15. b

CHAPTER 27: THE APOSTROPHE

Set 1

1. d	6. c	11. d
2. c	7. d	12. d
3. a	8. b	13. b
4. b	9. a	14. a
5. d	10. c	15. b

Set 2

1. a	6. a	11. c
2. c	7. c	12. a
3. d	8. d	13. d
4. b	9. a	14. a
5. a	10. c	15. b

CHAPTER 28: QUOTATION MARKS AND CAPITALIZATION

Set 1

1. d	6. d	11. d
2. c	7. b	12. b
3. a	8. c	13. d
4. c	9. d	14. b
5. d	10. a	15. c

Set 2

1. b	6. b	11. c
2. d	7. d	12. b
3. c	8. d	13. b
4. a	9. c	14. c
5. a	10. a	15. a

CHAPTER 29: EDITING PRACTICE

Set 1

1. d	6. a	11. a
2. a	7. a	12. a
3. c	8. b	13. c
4. b	9. d	14. b
5. d	10. a	15. c

Set 2

1. c	6. a	11. c
2. b	7. b	12. d
3. a	8. b	13. b
4. a	9. d	14. a
5. c	10. c	15. c